DEVIL'S ADVOCATES

DEVIL'S ADVOCATES is a series of books devoted to exploring the classics of horror cinema. Contributors to the series come from the fields of teaching, academia, journalism and fiction, but all have one thing in common: a passion for the horror film and a desire to share it with the widest possible audience.

'The admirable Devil's Advocates series is not only essential – and fun – reading for the serious horror fan but should be set texts on any genre course.'
Dr Ian Hunter, Reader in Film Studies, De Montfort University, Leicester

'Auteur Publishing's new Devil's Advocates critiques on individual titles... offer bracingly fresh perspectives from passionate writers. The series will perfectly complement the BFI archive volumes.' **Christopher Fowler,** *Independent on Sunday*

'Devil's Advocates has proven itself more than capable of producing impassioned, intelligent analyses of genre cinema... quickly becoming the go-to guys for intelligent, easily digestible film criticism.' ***HorrorTalk.com***

'Auteur Publishing continue the good work of giving serious critical attention to significant horror films.' ***Black Static***

 DevilsAdvocatesbooks

 DevilsAdBooks

ALSO AVAILABLE IN THIS SERIES

A Girl Walks Home Alone at Night Farshid Kazemi

Black Sunday Martyn Conterio

The Blair Witch Project Peter Turner

Blood and Black Lace Roberto Curti

The Blood on Satan's Claw David Evans-Powell

Candyman Jon Towlson

Cannibal Holocaust Calum Waddell

Carrie Neil Mitchell

The Company of Wolves James Gracey

The Conjuring Kevin J. Wetmore Jr.

Creepshow Simon Brown

Cruising Eugenio Ercolani & Marcus Stiglegger

The Curse of Frankenstein Marcus K. Harmes

Daughters of Darkness Kat Ellinger

Dead of Night Jez Conolly & David Bates

The Descent James Marriot

The Devils Darren Arnold

Don't Look Now Jessica Gildersleeve

The Evil Dead Lloyd Haynes

The Fly Emma Westwood

Frenzy Ian Cooper

Halloween Murray Leeder

House of Usher Evert Jan van Leeuwen

In the Mouth of Madness Michael Blyth

It Follows Joshua Grimm

Ju-on The Grudge Marisa Hayes

Let the Right One In Anne Billson

M Samm Deighan

Macbeth Rebekah Owens

The Mummy Doris V. Sutherland

Nosferatu Cristina Massaccesi

Peeping Tom Kiri Bloom Walden

Re-Animator Eddie Falvey

Repulsion Jeremy Carr

Saw Benjamin Poole

Scream Steven West

The Shining Laura Mee

Shivers Luke Aspell

The Silence of the Lambs Barry Forshaw

Suspiria Alexandra Heller-Nicholas

The Texas Chain Saw Massacre James Rose

The Thing Jez Conolly

Trouble Every Day Kate Robertson

Twin Peaks: Fire Walk With Me Lindsay Hallam

Witchfinder General Ian Cooper

FORTHCOMING

[REC] Jim Harper

Cape Fear Rob Daniel

Possession Alison Taylor

Devil's Advocates

Prevenge

Andrew Graves

Acknowledgements

Thanks to Alice Lowe without her help and assistance this book would not exist. Thanks also to Vaughan Sivell at Western Edge Pictures, John Atkinson at Auteur Publishing/LUP and my wife Anna Graves for her endless patience.

First published in 2021 by
Auteur, an imprint of
Liverpool University Press,
4 Cambridge Street,
Liverpool
L69 7ZU

Series design: Nikki Hamlett at Cassels Design
Set by Cassels Design, Luton UK

All rights reserved. No part of this publication may be reproduced in any material form (including photocopying or storing in any medium by electronic means and whether or not transiently or incidentally to some other use of this publication) without the permission of the copyright owner.

British Library Cataloguing-in-Publication Data
A catalogue record for this book is available from the British Library

ISBN paperback: 978-1-80085-594-6
ISBN hardback: 978-1-80085-593-9
ISBN epub: 978-1-80085-836-7
ISBN PDF: 978-1-80085-770-4

Contents

Introduction 7

Chapter 1: Delivery 9

Chapter 2: The Lowe Down 21

Chapter 3: Island of Terror 39

Chapter 4: Brat's Entertainment 53

Chapter 5: Mourning Gory 65

Chapter 6: Alice Through the Looking Glass 77

Chapter 7: Bleeding the Way 87

Sources 97

Introduction

From *Village of the Damned* (1960), *Rosemary's Baby* (1968), *The Omen* (1976) through to *Demon Seed* (1977) and *Alien* (1979), the manifestation of 'the monstrous child' has been explored in twentieth-century horror cinema on countless occasions. Fears that our children were, at least on a metaphorical level, turning into satanic creatures, emotionless extra-terrestrials or, as in the case of *I Was a Teenage Werewolf* (1957), slavering lycanthropes, have haunted the post-war silver screen for decades, becoming as potent a symbol of destruction as a flame breathing Godzilla stamping through Tokyo in atomic age Japan. Indeed, the bomb which fell on Hiroshima, providing the catalyst for that particular radioactive lizard, was called 'Little Boy'. But with *Prevenge* (2016) we are presented with a uniquely British take on that classic genre trope.

There is something so colourfully dark about Alice Lowe's directorial debut that it can, on first viewing, present us with the slightly awkward feeling of not knowing whether to laugh or hide behind the settee. Of course, we can always do both. Its unabashed horror and series of grisly murders are matched with an understated deadpan wit, which never descends into throwaway camp. Lowe, as troubled expectant mother Ruth, presents us with a pixie-faced grim reaper, waddling away from each blood drenched crime scene with casual indifference. On the surface, it's an interesting and entertaining revenge flick which subverts certain Hollywood clichés, but it is also an important slice of uniquely British cinema which explores modern inequality via the medium of low-budget slasher.

Whereas *The Exorcist* (1973) arguably sought to highlight growing parental concerns about rebellious offspring in the Vietnam, pot smoking deluge of the Watergate era, *Prevenge* becomes an up-to-date parable challenging misogyny and the 'inbred' lazy attitudes which pervade the confusing state of a post-Brexit un-United Kingdom. And as modern as it undoubtedly is, it also borrows heavily, albeit in its look and feel, rather than its more explicit social commentary, from UK horror movies of the late '60s and early '70s.

The purpose of this book is to examine the marrying together of children, parental anxiety and the role of mother in the twenty-first-century genre film. It will also explore the often played out gimmick of pregnancy as 'body horror'. *Prevenge* provides an excellent conduit to explore these issues and to make a study of such offerings, the female function in horror cinema and the uneasy social commentaries which ensue. Placing this and other work within a societal and a historical context will provide the backbone of this text.

It will explore *Prevenge*'s inception, narrative development, reception and cult film status, as well investigating the impetus of first-time director Lowe, detailing her previous work as writer and performer and her collaborations with other artists such as Ben Wheatley and Steve Oram.

In order to fully contextualise *Prevenge* and its relevance and its effectiveness within the genre it sits in, this book will seek to address certain relevant questions such as: What makes *Prevenge* a quintessentially British horror? How does it subvert male-led genre conventions? And what links and sets this apart from other female-led genre pieces such as *Possession* (1981) and the more recent *Hereditary* (2018)?

Prevenge is a British horror movie, an exploitation piece and a cleverly crafted narrative. It traverses the delicate line between comedy and a deeper sense of tragedy by fusing together a more naturalistic approach with grand set pieces and Dr Phibes-esque serial murders. It deconstructs the slasher film and the sexism therein by attacking both literally and metaphorically representations of misogyny and gender-based inequality. And yet it also remains a personal piece, a moving, if somewhat disturbing drama detailing the anxieties of motherhood, pregnancy and a woman's seeming inability to grieve in a conventionally acceptable manner. It's a production which feels happier in the morgue than the maternity ward and yet there is a humanity and an urgency there which forces us to examine our deeper set concerns about birth, life and death.

Chapter 1: Delivery

> The explosion of galaxies is violent. A comet falling on Jupiter making seven different holes is violent. The birth of a child is very violent…Life is violent, the circulation of blood, the heart beating, all is violent. But there are two types of violence, creative and destructive. I am creating art. Alejandro Jodorowksy

There's a scene in *Prevenge* in which heavily pregnant Ruth notices a little girl walking by. In similar moments in more traditional Hollywood-style productions we can imagine there being a second of recognition between the two strangers, a wave or the faintest of smiles perhaps, to show us that despite the protagonist's many crimes, her 'natural' maternal instincts will kick in to save her and the bond between adult female and infant will win out in the end. In the hands of Alice Lowe though, we are afforded no such comforts. Ruth does attempt a weak smile but cannot. She simply looks through the young child as though she were some sort of alien being. It's this kind of detail which sets Ruth and the story which she inhabits apart from every other 'monstrous child' film you are likely to have seen, or will see. As Lowe offers:

> …I think I wanted there to be this tension and I definitely wanted to strip away any of the audience's preconceptions about this woman being a mother. (Lowe, 2019)

Few could deny that she accomplished this with her directorial debut. In another moment, as if to underline the point, Ruth, after dispatching her first victim, Mr Zabek (Dan Renton Skinner), a slimy reptile of a man, literally strips away her mumsy disguise and burns it before our eyes. It's a symbolic cremation of clichéd cinematic motherhood and lets us know immediately that this particular murderous narrative will hold no truck with traditional depictions of maternity-frocked frailty. It's a funeral pyre for our unchallenged expectations, and it's a statement of intent.

Prevenge is littered with other such visual flourishes, stark social commentary and black-as-hell comedy. Like the more recent *Joker* (2019), it's a dark character study and a deeply unsettling journey into a lost soul. Indeed, *Joker* appears to mimic *Prevenge* on some levels, the tragic physical transformation from Arthur Fleck (Joaquin Phoenix) to his violent alter ego, where the character applies his white face-paint before going full on psychopath, echoing Ruth's own pre-Halloween night murderous excursion. Accidental or otherwise, both sequences are markedly similar in their approach in demonstrating a protagonist's final move toward out-and-out insanity.

Image #1 – Joaquin Phoenix, Joker (2019) © Warner Bros.

Image #2 – Alice Lowe, Prevenge (2016) © Western Edge Pictures

The story of *Prevenge* is essentially that of Ruth (Alice Lowe), who, when she is left heavily pregnant and alone, embarks on a vicious killing spree to wipe out those she sees as being responsible for the death of her partner, and father of her unborn child. This is no ordinary foetus, though. We are led to believe that our protagonist is somehow being controlled from the womb, that she is capable of entering into dialogue with her female baby and it is these pre-natal conversations which send her on a chaotic bloodstained journey. The infant voice from 'within' urges Ruth to become 'Ruth-less' in just one of the many instances where Lowe equates the idea of pregnancy with 'loss of self'.

Only learning of her pregnancy on the same day that her partner died in a tragic climbing incident, Ruth, decides to enact a grisly series of retribution murders which she carries out between visits to her concerned midwife. Her victims are the fellow climbers who, when given the choice of saving their own lives or that of Ruth's partner, chose the former, cutting the umbilical-style rope which held them together ensuring that he would plunge to his death. Tracking her prey by means of social media and other methods, Ruth exacts her revenge on each member of the group.

These include DJ Dan (Tom Davis), a chauvinist cliché, Ella (Kate Dickie), a hard-nosed business woman, who has her face smashed against a see-through table in a mocking allusion to glass ceiling limitations, Zac (Tom Meeten), an arty middle-class flat owner who has a Buddha statue shoved through his eyeball, and Len (Gemma Whelan), a wide-eyed fitness obsessive who's kick boxing skills prove no match for Ruth's vengeful blade. It is only when she closes in on final target Tom (Kayvan Novak), the climbing instructor, that her plans start to unravel. She gate-crashes Tom's Halloween party but as she is about to execute him, she hesitates, when she becomes aware that his partner is also heavily pregnant; not only this, her waters break and she is rushed into hospital. After undergoing an emergency caesarean section, Ruth, presented with her child, seems crestfallen when she realises it is not the demon girl she has imagined but '…just a normal little baby'. Ruth seems to acknowledge that she has made a terrible mistake carrying out her murderous activities.

Later, Ruth returns once again to the clifftops still haunted by the ghost of her dead partner. Once there, she runs into Tom. For a second they exchange glances, there seems to be an unspoken agreement between them but in the final moments Ruth raises her arms and screams like a deranged banshee. Tom has not escaped her merciless campaign. Ruth has chosen death over birth.

In part, *Prevenge* riffs on old horror tropes, those of the demon child or possessed mother. As mentioned above, it's an angle which has been played out in numerous incarnations from *The Omen* to *The Exorcist*, but what sets it apart from those earlier films, particularly *Rosemary's Baby* and *Village of Damned*, is its unflinching ability to place this female protagonist with all her tragic flaws, criminality and brutality, at the heart of the story. While Rosemary Woodhouse might be the focus of our attention in Polanski's classic, we are never asked to question her reasoning; she is of course the victim or vessel, a put-upon conveyor of the Devil's child. Yet, even when she is confronted by her Hell-spawned offspring, her unquestioned motherly protection is never in doubt. Not so with *Prevenge*, as Lowe states:

> I wanted to get rid of any ideas of like softness, mercy, clemency, kindness…[Ruth] hasn't got any of those things. So, don't expect those things from her just because she's a mum. (Lowe, 2019)

It is Lowe's use of doubt within Ruth's mind which is most interesting and disturbing. Her reason and reasoning shift throughout the film's tight narrative. At first Ruth appears to have some semblance of power over her unborn child, but the battle rages within and towards the end of the film it is clear that she is losing her grip: 'I'm not in control. I don't want to know what's in there. I'm scared of her.' This is unintentionally rammed home by the well-meaning midwife when she innocently tells Ruth that she will have '…absolutely no control over your mind and body'. This changing state of affairs is brought to bear in the way that Ruth dispatches her victims. At first there is a hint of uncertainty, regret, a feeling that she is doing wrong but somehow compelled to do so. During her encounter with DJ Dan, for instance, she appears to be trying to give him an 'out', by questioning him about his intentions she seems to be affording him a chance; but of course, Dan being the selfish and unthinking brute that he is, fails to pick up on that and he is inelegantly done away with.

But as her campaign goes on she becomes more callous and efficient. However, unlike the character arc of other 'screen monsters' hers is an ever-wavering one, a visual metaphor for the changes inflicted on the pregnant body. She is capable of being monstrous *and* human, making the horror of the situation more disconcerting. This is underlined when she plants a kiss on the forehead of her victims once they have been killed.

This alarming and un-Hollywood approach to maternity is rammed home most devastatingly when Ruth tells her increasingly concerned mid-wife that she would 'swap her to have him back', meaning that unlike Rosemary, her instincts do not automatically lead to her needing to protect her unborn child without question, particularly if she were given the option of getting back her dead partner.

With a film like *Village of the Damned*, we are presented with a disturbing 1960s science fiction piece which, though tackling the idea of alien impregnation – a uniquely female experience – never looks at this nightmarish scenario from that viewpoint, its set of women characters being sidelined for more middle-aged male responses to the growing crisis. Lowe, though, explores pregnancy solely through the eyes of a troubled female protagonist, exposing this 'natural' state of affairs in all its gory detail. She skilfully links all the fears and transformations one experiences during this process and moulds them together in a story which is more in line with Ridley Scott's *Alien* or Cronenberg's many takes on the body horror sub-genre, than other more genteel presentations of human gestation. As she says:

> It was important to me to portray a pregnant woman from the inside out, rather than the outside in. Many of my favourite films, *Rosemary's Baby* etc., depict, I think, with an onlooker's gaze, probably a male gaze. The mother is vulnerable, sweet, helpless, loving. There's no sense of existential angst, questioning motherhood itself. What it does to the body, the mind, the identity. These are all assumed as things women should take for granted, as 'normal', 'natural'. (Lowe, 2019)

The gestation period for the actual film though, in comparison to the lengthy 'development hell' torments of many projects, was mercifully short and in some respects, it was born out of a slightly tetchy exchange Lowe had had with director Jamie Adams. Lowe had worked with Adams on the low-budget *Black Mountain Poets* (2015). Coming at a low point in her career, after Ben Wheatley's *Sightseers* (2012), when she had 'won some awards then…nothing', it made a welcome change and though the filming schedule seemed impossibly tight, she literally had nothing else to lose. And yet, the experience proved to be more valuable than she had expected:

> I think it flexed loads of muscles that I didn't know I had. Improvisation, but also writing on the hoof, thinking ahead about audience reaction, plot, dialogue, all at the last minute. And by throwing me into that deep end, Jamie gave me loads of insight into my own abilities. (Lowe, 2019)

But it was later, when she was 'five months up the duff' and still reeling from a stalled Film4 production, that Adams approached her about another potential project.

Touting the idea that she should write something for another actor, he was met with an understandably grumpy response from Lowe, already despairing at the industry.

> Jamie, if I am going to write a fucking vehicle for Cara Delevigne, I am gonna do it for £50K from Working Title, not 50 pence from you. If I am going to work myself to the bone whilst heavily pregnant for no money, it will be a project FOR and ABOUT me. (Lowe, 2019)

To her surprise, Adams agreed and Lowe was tasked with writing and directing a film while heavily pregnant. She had been mulling over ideas about mothers and motherhood both personally and professionally. But it was only when she was faced with the prospect of becoming one, that she came up with the idea of *Prevenge*, which as she admitted later, grew out of a sort of 'hormonal paranoia'. It was at this point that Western Edge Pictures became aware of the potential project. As producer Vaughan Sivell recalls:

> A sort of friend of an acquaintance that we'd been working with at the time had said that Alice was looking to direct her first movie, and so we arranged to meet her. And she came along and said she'd been in development with various other people for a long time on things that hadn't come off. She was about to have a baby and she was worried about when she would get to make her first film. But she had a good idea, and she knew that we were a company that could just sort of make it happen quickly. I'd always been a big fan of hers, got on well with her and I said 'Have you got a script?' and she said 'No but I've got a few good ideas' and I think that must have been in the September, early September, and basically, we had finished shooting by Christmas. (Sivell, 2019)

Western Edge was unfazed by the prospect of working with a heavily pregnant writer/actor/director, awestruck by Lowe's talent, commitment and impressive work ethic. *Prevenge* was written, developed and shot in the tiny window of just four months. Yet while the process was uncommonly quick, according to Sivell:

> It recognisably went through every stage of development that all scripts go through, it just happened really, really quick because Alice writes really fast because she had the unstoppable deadline of having her baby to push her on. (Sivell, 2019)

Originally pitched as a sort of female *Taxi Driver* (1976), Lowe took some of those 1970s anti-hero pictures as inspiration, tapping not only into their material but also into how those films were made and looked. Though slightly apprehensive about directing her first low budget feature on location in Cardiff, in the late autumn of 2015, Lowe was also aware that there were certain freedoms in terms of content and significance, which may have been stifled on a more expensive shoot.

As director, Lowe was able to meticulously plan her operation, deciding to plump originally for an eight-day shoot, (this also included 3 pick up days, so 11 in total), incorporating lengthier two hander sequences to cut back on location filming and actors. And while there were limitations in terms of budget, Lowe was quick to realise how the prospect of private funding, small as it might be, may play to her advantage. As she states:

> The film cost so little that there was really no one to answer to. The first draft was pretty much the last draft. With a few tweaks. Which gave me loads of trust in my own judgement. And loads of mistrust in 'development processes'. I now find all my work is about avoiding them. Because they can destroy a good film! (Lowe, 2019)

It's also important to recognise this debut as being more than just the product of work-a-day direction in a time-precious environment. *Prevenge* is a remarkable exemplar of twenty-first-century British filmmaking on the hoof. Its combination of uncompromising yet tight storytelling, neatly captured performances and dark subject matter, framed by the expert eye of Lowe and her cinematographer Ryan Eddleston, make for a visually arresting, challenging and ultimately entertaining ninety-minute showcase. Its down-to-earth, almost kitchen sink textures juxtapose with its more lavish flourishes such as the often talked about Halloween sequence, which sees Ruth decked out in flowing red frock and Day of the Dead style black and white greasepaint, taking to the crowded Cardiff streets like an expectant angel of death. It also carefully balances horror with comedy, symbolism with matter-of-fact imagery, tragedy, biting satire and well-engineered narrative structure. Take the opening images for example: vertigo inducing views over clifftops lead us down to the sea below where waves crash against the shoreline. Flashback glimpses of some frayed climbing rope and blood spilled on the rocks intercut with glimpses of a dour-looking protagonist. It's a grim montage which not only embeds within it neat foreshadowing of the story about to unfold but also cleverly constructed references to childbirth-linked metaphor – the umbilical-like broken rope being an explicit observation of Ruth's state of mind and how, through rage and grief, she has cut herself free of accepted convention, and has rejected her place within normal society. Take also the idea of Ruth 'playing' different characters in the lead up to dispatching her victims. The disguises, from a narrative sense, make it easier for her to lure her prey in believably, and yet they also, according to Lowe, tap into more symbolic anxieties around an expectant mother's *loss of self*.

> From my perspective having Ruth as a grieving woman was a really useful metaphor for someone grieving the loss of their own identity. The idea of motherhood as 'the death of the self'. There's so many people telling you, 'life will never be the same again, YOU will never be the same again'. I found it absolutely petrifying. Like, 'will I wake up the next morning and be a different person? Like a Stepford Wife? (Lowe, 2019)

Above all, *Prevenge* perhaps works best because it urges us to imagine this world via Ruth's point of view. Although her actions are repellent, we can at least see the relevance of them, feel the pain which she dulls by carrying out this sequence of homicides. Ruth is no Michael Myers, Freddie Kruger or Jason and that's the point; she's more real than that, which makes her a far more disquieting and ultimately a more tragic prospect.

Each element from co-actor, location and colour fits perfectly into the package Lowe presents us with, especially in the beautifully arranged score provided by Toydrum which weaves through new wave beats and mournful passages with an urgent and distinctive on-message soundscape channelling Goblin, John Carpenter and early electronica. Lowe had worked with the pair (Pablo Clements and James Griffiths) before on short film *Solitudo* (2014) and was impressed by the outfit's approach.

> What's great about them is that they're so film literate and they have the same taste in films as I do, so if I say '*Cannibal Holocaust*' to them, they're like 'Yeah, yeah, yeah'. So, any gaps I have in music knowledge I can bridge by saying 'Yeah but do you know this film soundtrack?'... They work in a really organic way and it's the way I like to work. You find good people, and you kind of ask them to use their instincts and don't overly hover over every choice they're making. The stuff they did for the Halloween walk, for example. They created a piece and then they laid it on top of the edit and it worked

immediately. I was like, 'Oh my God'. It just worked so amazingly well. (Lowe, 2019)

Previewed initially at festivals including London Film Festival, Toronto International Film Festival and Venice Film Festival, at the back end of 2016, *Prevenge* wouldn't go on to general release till February 2017 in the UK and Ireland before trailing across the rest of the world in the months to follow. It was met with much critical acclaim. The *New York Times* opined that:

> …what hoists this bloody battiness above much of the scrappily low-budget horror pack is the smartness of its execution and the strength of the movie's central performance. As Ruth, a profoundly lonely expectant mother, Alice Lowe (who also wrote and directed) personifies weaponized gestation. (Catsoulis, 2017)

While *The Guardian*'s Peter Bradshaw made note of the multi-layered possibilities of the film's intriguing title:

> The movie appears, on the face of it, to be a straightforward story of revenge. But *Prevenge* could also be a way of getting your retaliation in first, a pre-emptive payback for all the bad things that each victim is presumed capable of doing. (Bradshaw, 2016)

But while *Prevenge* certainly avails itself to more intellectual discussions of horror, it could also, in some respects, appeal to the previous fans of films like *Sightseers* and possibly even *Shaun of the Dead* (2004). Its marketing campaign and trailer play heavily on its use of dark humour and more salacious elements. The main poster image, for example, features a slightly playful Lowe, swathed in a shroud-like dress, one hand on her pregnant belly, the other holding a serious-looking blade behind her back, making the tagline below, 'Killing for Two', both pithy and absurd. Yet the image is also loaded, and while it might be said that it fails to capture fully the more serious tone on first glance, it does, once viewed more closely, provide us with a clever shorthand to Lowe/Ruth's obsession with loss, nihilism and rejection of traditional views of motherhood. Lowe toys with concepts of life and death both balanced figuratively on a knife-edge, the violence and pain of child birth implicit in the *Masque of The Red Death* choice of ghastly maternity garb.

Image #3 – Poster for Prevenge (2016) © Western Edge Pictures

Given the niche charm and its controversial nature, it was never quite going to appeal to the same sort of fanboy audience as Shaun of the Dead, with its more easily marketable zombie shtick; and subsequently Prevenge's gross worldwide box office takings to date are limited, though not unrespectable (around £84,000/$104,000).

Prevenge was perhaps always destined for the more arthouse-style scene. The premise feels more like the kind of story one might find in an underground alternative comic book than a mainstream movie and Lowe herself feels less like a 'star' and more like an epigrammatic conduit for her personal brand of twisted tales. She radiates a sort of deadpan joy which bizarrely works effectively in comedy, horror or kids' telly. When looking at Lowe's face it is often hard to tell whether she is about admonish the world around it with a deeply cutting remark or collapse in a fit of girlish giggles. It is not a sense of fame or stardom which Lowe most exudes, rather it is her uncanny ability to be both completely honest and utterly mysterious at the same time.

But arguably this film seems to fit best in the 'cult' rather than the more easily accessible populist arena. Its uneasy tension, humour and uniquely British outlook lend the production a peculiar sensibility which appears to draw more (at least in its use of 'Little England' oddness) from older works like The Abominable Doctor Phibes (1971) or Theatre of Blood (1973) than it does from more recent efforts like Se7en (1995) or Zodiac (2007). But Prevenge transcends the level of simply being quirky (a term that Lowe is quick to dismiss) and backs this up with something more solidly profound.

While its murderous set pieces appear to exist in a sort of woozy unreality, its humanity is set at a deeper level. It is Ruth's unbearable sense of loss, despair and blank-faced communication with an equally uncaring world full of misogynists, lechers, cowards and cold-hearted capitalists, that we are most responsive to. With *Prevenge* it could be argued that we are not just tapping into Alice Lowe's imagination: on some level we are tapping into a part of Alice Lowe.

> I look back and actually I think I had been repressing making stuff about my own life (not that I go around killing people but…). I think Jordan Peele said something similar in an interview, something along the lines of, 'it took me a while to realise that the more painful, the more truthful the work, the better it is'. Maybe that's to do with coming from a comedy background where often comedy masks pain with a kind of Teflon bravado. But *Prevenge* fully forced me out of that comfort zone. Suddenly I was making something uncomfortably close to what was happening to me, albeit psychologically rather than via my actions. And that made it a really cathartic and important evolution for me personally and professionally. (Lowe, 2019)

So, who on Earth is she?

Chapter 2: The Lowe Down

> I'm really interested in dream perspectives, in that cinema is just a dream, a projection of someone's dream…Everything I write is about madness to a degree. What is reality, what is time?' (Lowe, 2019)

The discerning, or even undiscerning, British TV viewer would be hard pushed not to have caught at least two or three Alice Lowe appearances over the last fifteen years or so. Her credits both as star and guest include *My Life in Film* (2004), *Annually Retentive* (2006-2007), *Beehive* (2008), *Comedy Lab* (2001), *Sherlock* (2014) *Ruddy Hell! It's Harry and Paul* (2007-2012), *Skins* (2012), *The Mighty Boosh* (2005), *Snuff Box* (2006), *The IT Crowd* (2006) and, of course, Garth Marenghi's *Dark Place* (2004) (on which more later). In some respects, she is the quintessential character actor but also, as this book is attempting to demonstrate, something much more.

> I've never considered myself a conventional 'actress', whatever that means. I never played Juliet or whatever. I always saw acting as a creative medium, a means to tell a story. And it takes less practice than piano, and I'm quite lazy so… But I enjoy 'making things', telling stories. I like that acting means you can make something out of nothing, create ideas out of empty space. (Lowe, 2019)

One thing that leaps out when watching or listening to Alice Lowe's work and that becomes particularly clear when talking to her in person, is her absolute conviction in the project she is engaged in, be it a smaller acting role, writing, central performance, direction or even live Q&A or interview. Her ability to mix a serious dedication to her art with a sparky sense of humour and refreshing lack of ego, make her an appealing prospect as both creative persona and study. Her appearances in more well-known material such as the hugely popular children's educational television show *Horrible Histories* (2010-2011), or her inclusion in episodes of *Black Mirror: Bandersnatch* (2018) or *Inside No.9* (2015) somehow seem to complement her more unorthodox work in short film and live performance. Being able to shift focus so easily from more avant-garde output like spoof folk act Hot Brew and her links with The Velvet Onion alternative comedy network, to more mainstream efforts might weaken the USP of other creative types, their 'brand' somehow being lost in that catch-all phrase of 'the jobbing actor'. Yet Lowe somehow thrives on this hyperactivity, outwardly exuding a sort of dogged perfectionist and wild-eyed experimenter, becoming simultaneously both conscientious lab technician and a manic Dr Frankenstein.

In some ways, it might be said that there are parallels between Lowe and fifties professional weirdo Vampira. Vampira, an over the top horror queen persona, played by daughter of a Finnish immigrant Maila Nurmi, became a brief yet highly controversial star of American television in an age of growing atomic fears and where women were being coaxed back into the kitchen with a never-ending wave of television commercials, government propaganda, and media outlets, that sought to smash the independent feminist spirit which had developed during the labour-short years of the Second World War. This situation – the 'Rosie the Riveter paradox' – is best summed up by author, podcaster and film historian Karina Longworth:

> Women were expected to go to work when women were at war, and in so doing so they learned what it felt like to exchange their own labour for a pay cheque, and they learned what it felt like to not be dependent on a man for all of their material needs. Then, having had that experience, at the end of the war they were expected to revert back their previous roles often as housewives with no real purpose outside of the home and in some cases the genie couldn't be put back into the bottle. The woman didn't want to go back in time, back to a life of comparatively few freedoms. A life of comfort perhaps but also one of servitude. Once they'd been given a chance to have an identity outside the home, they couldn't just give it up…(Longworth, 2018)

The Vampira Show was, on the surface, an entertaining connective tissue which played out between screenings of late-night scary movies. However, Nurmi, a subversive with a wittily sharp intellect, used the platform to create a satire on the modern way of life, particularly the stereotype of the American housewife. Vampira was a fiendishly dark comic figure who predated *The Addams Family* TV show, Lilly Munster or indeed a host of Gothic phantoms like Siouxsie Sioux who came along later in the 1970s and early '80s. She wore heavy black eye make-up over deathly white foundation, a vampire bat wing dress and fishnets stockings, and her already tiny waist was drawn in by a ridiculously restrictive corset, the exaggerated distortion a mockery of male-preferred female fashions. As W. Scott Poole described in his excellent biography *Vampira*:

> Vampira screamed. She screamed instead of cleaning the house, washing the dishes, of falling in love with appliances. She screamed rebellion, a challenge to the high walls of containment and a symbolic middle finger raised toward the popular representation of the housewife…Nurmi's Vampira was a ghoulish incarnation of a wave of rebellion. The idea that something could be both outlandish in order to be truthful, that it had to be outlandish in order to be truthful, represented an idea just coming out of the American closet in the mid-50s. (Poole, 2014, 18-19)

That notion of something being outlandish in order to be truthful and vice versa is something that also exudes from Lowe and her cast of characters whether it's Tina from *Sightseers* or Ruth in *Prevenge*, and while neither of those is as bombastic as a Vampira persona, there is, particularly in the former, something which seems to sit in the shadow of Maila Nurmi's nightmare satire. Just as Vampira cut across the accepted norms of femininity and the housewife, Lowe seems to cut across the accepted notions of modern woman and mother, the swollen body, red dress and blade becoming as transgressive as Nurmi's deformed waist and monstrous demeanour.

Born in Coventry, Alice Eva Lowe seemed to unleash her creative side fairly early on, given space within the family set-up to explore her more artistic, if slightly bizarre childish fascinations.

> I was very into drawing and making stuff as a kid, and had quite a few weird interests. My mum is very artistic and so encouraged this. I made a small shrine to Jesus in an old medicine cabinet my mum gave me. You slid the mirror back and there was a Bible, Jesus on the cross, candles, the works. So that was quite weird. Jesus was a pin up to me, it wasn't really religious. I liked *Jesus Christ Superstar*, and the New Testament. And I think I thought Jesus was just something you could get into like skating or hockey. I also made a small fossil museum under my bed that you could pay 50p to see by shining at it with a torch. I'm very grateful I didn't have the internet or I wouldn't have done any of these weird things. I also made a house for some toy mice that wore clothes, and my mum and dad recently found a book where I had written about these mice's adventures, shopping, birthday parties and the suchlike. At the end, they were all massacred in a bloodbath. I did think, 'hmm, that sounds about right', although I didn't really remember writing it. I think my mum and dad were

> amused but ever so slightly concerned in retrospect that it's evidence for me being a psychopath. (Lowe, 2019)

She quickly developed an appetite for books and other forms of literature healthily devouring the likes of Roald Dahl, CS Lewis, Jane Austen, Dickens and any ghost stories she could lay her hands on. Her absorption of these types of texts was clearly having an impact on her developing creative psyche.

> So, while I was all spotty and miserable and weird at school, I was building my imagination at home in my own strange sanctuary of Venetian masks and hand crocheted fingerless gloves. (Lowe, 2019)

It is Lowe's fascination with stories and storytelling which perhaps most influenced her later creative impulses. When considering the lot of younger people, now including her first daughter, Della, she is quick to warn against the dangers of children drifting away from the idea of actual literature and telling tales.

> I do sometimes look at my daughter, obviously, she already knows what YouTube is and she's obsessed with it. And I'm just a bit like 'Aw, you're just watching guff already, you're not watching anything that's really going to nail in and embed as this fantastic thing'. I'm always just going 'please just watch stories', instead of a tutorial on how to make a cake that looks like a Disney character. (Lowe, 2019)

The dominance of dark fantasy and horror, which was making its way onto the tiny portable TV Lowe had begged her parents to buy for her in order to have late-night access to those often forbidden small-screen treasures, was clearly having an impact too. TV shows like *Jim Henson's The Storyteller* and films like *The Dark Crystal* (1982), *Krull* (1983), *Return to Oz* (1985) and *Labyrinth* (1986) became an important part of her existence as did the presence of the latter movie's star, David Bowie, who would prove vital in Lowe's musical education, and a handy distraction to more formal learning institutions. Though quite outgoing at middle school, she seemed to struggle later, as she states:

> I quickly went entirely into my shell at secondary school, as I suddenly felt my nerd status elevate a billion degrees. Somehow, I had got away with it before. Dunno why, I was into Jesus for pity's sake. And I was rubbish at sports. So, I retreated into myself,

> and mainly listened to my parents' old vinyl while gazing morosely at pre-Raphelite postcards and drawing Medusa. Music has always been massive for me. Kate Bush, Bowie, Cat Stevens, Fleetwood Mac, then later Madonna and Prince and Björk. I think that was what really got me into the idea of transformation, being more than one character, choosing personae and using them to build worlds. These multi-disciplinarians who seemingly could control their own reality/exist within fantasy. (Lowe, 2019)

Regardless of her difficulties fitting in during her formative years, Lowe was able to gain a place at Kings College, Cambridge. It was here that Lowe really developed a sense of what she might be able to achieve in terms of performance.

> I went in for a meeting for a student play, to design some costumes (which is what I thought I might want to do for a living), and went out with an acting role. (Lowe, 2019)

Though drawn to creativity and performance, she was fully expectant that it would remain a hobby, but her skillset led her to devising a handful of experimental theatre shows such as *City Haunts*, *Snowbound* and *Progress in Flying Machines*, alongside future *Peep Show* stars David Mitchell and Robert Webb, under the direction of Paul King. The latter remains a hugely influential figure in Lowe's life, forever awakening her to the idea that '…you can change, evolve, develop into the person you want to be'. Feeling the pressure to comply with her dismayed parents' requests to get a 'proper job', Lowe found herself teaching English to foreign language students 'at this totally rubbish place' on Oxford Street. Though clearly Lowe's distinctive presence and style would be the impetus behind *Prevenge*, that Alice Lowe-ness took a while to find its place within the creative and highly competitive landscape. According to her, the need to keep working and maintaining an individuality can be a difficult burden to bear even now, and has been throughout her career.

> It is a really difficult line to tread and I think I'm quite conscious now…you've got to have your feet in both camps, I think, a little bit. You've got to have different levels to your work where someone can take it as a straightforward slasher film or a straightforward comedy, or whatever but also they can take it deeper if they want to. That way you're pleasing the money people but…there's something intelligent about

it, it's got some integrity to it. Having said that, for a while I think I fell down a gap because of that. I always have that bit in my work that is sort of populist, I don't go out of my way to be weird, I want people to watch my work. And at the moment, things like *Parasite* winning an Oscar and stuff, I'm like, you know, I don't think my stuff is that weird. It's becoming mainstream now. In the past I was making these short films and they were funny but they were also sort of artistic and we would really struggle to get them into film festivals and stuff, or we would struggle to get interest because people would be like 'Well, it's funny but it's not funny enough and there's this weird bit in it. And there's this bit that makes us feel scared or sad', or whatever. Then on the other hand it was too commercial to be an arthouse short film. So, we'd sort of be in the middle where I'd be going 'Isn't that good that we're doing both things?' But it was like *no* because we were sort of in between. And again, I would say what's happened with Netflix now and a lot of TV stuff where there's a lot of merging of genres, stuff is funny and sad and scary or whatever. That's the way stuff has gone anyway, so it's sort of okay. But I think for a long time people didn't know where to put us. When I was doing these short films with Jaqueline Wright it was really frustrating because we'd be going, 'What we're doing's great!' And it *was* great but I think perhaps a bit ahead of the curve and people didn't know what to do with it. (Lowe, 2019)

But this idea of being weird without meaning to be weird possibly found its place within the initial *Garth Marenghi* stage shows *Fright Knight* and *Netherhead*. Lowe would appear in both productions and the subsequent critical acclaim they garnered meant she could finally escape the far-from-satisfactory teaching position she was having to hold down.

…it was a joy when I could go in and tell my boss, 'I'm going on tour and I'm not coming back.' This was for the *Garth Marenghi* stage show. And we'd just won the Perrier award, which meant I was going to get paid and everything. I remember my boss was a kind of embittered former filmmaker/comedian and he basically had said to me, 'Give up on your dreams because if it was going to happen it would have happened by now.' So, it was pretty satisfying to walk out of that job. (Lowe, 2019)

In 2004 that stage show was adapted for Channel 4. *Garth Marenghi's Dark Place* was a multi-layered piece of meta-fictional TV, incorporating the 'show within a show' idea but taking it further through the looking glass than other series had ever before attempted.

Written by and starring Matthew Holness it incorporated deliberately dated low-budget video footage with pretentious early noughties retrospective talking head interviews. The whole production played out as both wilfully silly and deceptively clever. Though lasting only one series, the show remains fondly remembered by critics and its army of cult followers but to the uninitiated it is not the easiest of concepts to explain.

The basic premise is that *Garth Marenghi's Dark Place* is a never-before-aired TV show. Each 'lost' episode is presented by Garth Marenghi (Matthew Holness) who also stars in the show within the show, as Dr Rick Dagless MD. Marenghi, who describes himself in the gloriously recreated vintage opening credits as 'author, dream weaver, visionary, plus actor', is a well observed and typically ludicrous example of the kind of narcissist male horror writer that had emerged at the beginning of the early '80s, seemingly cut from the same bloodied cloth as now largely forgotten authors like Shawn Hutson, etc.

Each episode, intercut with interviews and commentary from its beleaguered cast of terrible actors, supposedly carries (at least according to Marenghi and his sycophantic publisher Dean Learner), a deep and meaningful message, which the squares at Channel 4 were apparently too squeamish to broadcast. The attention to detail, replete with dodgy editing, hilariously bad special effects and slightly out of synch voice dubs, plays with our woozy remembrance of '70s and '80s fare like *Tales of the Unexpected* (1979-1988), *Doctor Who* (1963-1989) and *Blake's 7* (1978-1981), willing us to blend our realities with this carefully constructed un-reality. It was a conceit later copied and used in 'The Devil of Christmas', the very funny yet deeply disturbing seasonal episode of the Reece Shearsmith and Steve Pemberton-scripted series *Inside No.9* (2012-) broadcast in December 2016.

When constructing the 'fake' series, Holness and crew employed a 'Monster of the Week' format, lacing it with Marenghi's crudely imagined use of analogy and aggressively idiotic handling of issues like AIDs, sex, racism and sexuality. The gang, consisting of Thornton Reed (Richard Ayoade), Dr Lucien Sanchez (Matt Berry), Marenghi (Holness) and Dr Liz Asher (Lowe), take on each new challenge with a deadpan stupidity that falls somewhere between *Kingdom Hospital* and *Scooby Doo*.

It is interesting to note, however, that, by exploiting his own alter ego's ineptitude with metaphor and political correctness, Holness, through his fake narrative, is able to intelligently explore issues such as gender inequality and misogyny. Lowe, who plays the gang's token 'girl', the occasionally psychic blonde bimbo Liz, cranks up the dead-eyed fluffiness of the character to the max, highlighting the inherent casting-couch scenarios of times past and the continued sexism therein. But it is perhaps the absence of Madeleine Wool, the actress who plays Dr Asher (also played by Lowe), which is the most telling. Unlike her male counterparts, who appear as talking heads in the retrospective elements of the show, Madeleine is nowhere to be seen, having disappeared in strange circumstances some time ago. Though obviously portrayed for laughs, viewed now in a post-#MeToo world, the storyline arguably plays out a little more uneasily.

Though fans were denied more than just the first run of six episodes and subsequent DVD release, members of the original cast would wind their way into other cult favourites or in some cases much more mainstream offerings. Co-creator Richard Ayoade (Dean Learner/Thorton Reed), would go on to star in the Graham Lineham comedy *The IT Crowd* (2006-2013) before writing and directing films like *Submarine* (2010) and *The Double* (2013), while Matt Berry (Todd Rivers/Dr. Lucian Sanchez) would continue to deconstruct the sitcom format with oddball shows like *Toast of London* (2012-2018) and *Year of the Rabbit* (2019). The show's other creator and star Holness decided to concentrate on writing and, after experimenting with ideas from Freud's essay 'The Uncanny', eventually wrote and directed his first feature, the terrifyingly bleak *Possum* (2018). Lowe, the show's only regular female cast member, would continue to work picking up roles in various TV and cinematic projects. But it was perhaps in another medium that she began to fully experiment with writing and performance, stretching her imagination to its limits unhindered by constraints or budgetary concerns.

Penned and starring Lowe, *Alice's Wunderland* was a bizarre and imaginative audio production which was aired on BBC Radio 4 between 2011 and 2015. The eponymous Wunderland – 'the Poundland of magical realms' – became an excellent conduit for Lowe's distinctly off-kilter view of the world and its occupants, but for the listener it also became a direct pipeline into the weird and wonderful headspace of its creator.

There aren't many spaces where you can be experimental and still get paid for it.

> Again, looking back, I see it as an important phase in me developing my confidence as a creative and a writer. Because I had a lot of freedom. There's also something about writing by oneself, even though I was creating lots of characters and 'worlds', they are all me! No getting away from it. Really that was the point of the name of the show, that it's a little journey around my mind. (Lowe, 2019)

In shorthand, *Alice's Wunderland* might be described as a sketch show, and in essence that's what it is, yet its presentation and use of soundscapes, editing, oral storytelling and world building result in something far less formulaic than other more recognisable examples of the genre. Its dizzy and slightly delirious delivery incorporating apocalyptic landscapes, dystopias and strangely terrifying Bizarro versions of oddly familiar children's material, help create a world of misfits, idiots and David Bowie-style 'scary monsters'. However, among the psychedelic assortment of freakishly random characters, pop culture references and nods to 'real life' characters such as Werner Herzog, Nico or even Steve McDonald from *Coronation Street*, can be discerned more regular fixtures. There is Nathan, for example, a sort of ASBO kid fever dream, his scatter fire blasts of dialogue detailing his daily juvenile delinquency, playing out like some wildly hypnotic drum 'n' bass track. Then there is the '70s Child Ghost', struck down as a youngster by the sort of tragic accident that only seemed to happen to kids in UK government-sponsored Public Information Films, who now wanders Wunderland, a creepy lost soul bemoaning his lonely existence, badly out-of-date haircut and lack of girlfriend:

> The saddest thing about being a child ghost is that I'll never get a girlfriend. There was a girl with bunches watching me be electrocuted on the pylon all those years ago, who grew up to be Lynda something or other from the *Birds of a Feather*. I remember looking at her in those final moments smelling singeing sneakers in the air, thinking that's the sort of girl I'd like to marry one day. Maybe she'll come and watch me play football in the rain wearing a scarf. She's the type of girl I'd like to see with a perm, you know, marriage material, but then halfway through me being electrocuted she ran off.

But what marks out Lowe's *Wunderland* so completely from other radio comedies is its experimental nature and its unquestionably British sensibility. Like all the smartest examples of UK counter-culture it manages to blend the exotic with the ordinary, the psychedelic with the banal. The show not only gives one a glimpse into Lowe's magical and unpredictable mind-set, where 'there is no such thing as a bad idea', it also affords one an insight into the writer's more obvious influences and inspirations, whether they be Radiophonic Workshop pioneer Delia Derbyshire, 1970s Public Information Films, *The Moomins* (1977-1982) or even Stanley Unwin. The latter is paid homage to via the confused utterings of the dizzy-headed narrator played by Marcia Warren. But beyond the more obvious influences it is clear that the show, like much of Lowe's work, flows along via the undercurrent of British oddity, the same indescribable stream which previously bought us Vic Reeves, Monty Python, Alan Moore, Ziggy Stardust, Ivor Cutler, *The League of Gentlemen* (1999-2017), Hammer horror and *Tales of the Unexpected*. It is Lowe's ability to utilise that UK idiosyncrasy as well as its rainy-island kitchen sink credentials, that arguably really informs her work – it's the acid tab dropped in the builder's tea. She astutely sums it up thus:

> There's an inherent sensibility in Britishness that does not fear its own weirdness and revels in its own low status. That was one of the instincts behind *Sightseers*, to make something that is essentially an American genre, but without any glamour whatsoever. The small, the negligible, tiny nuances, intonations, gestures, petty habituations, fondnesses, trinkets, and grudges. It's the stuff of Britishness isn't it? We're kind of a nation of emotional hoarders…

Alice's Wunderland in a sense, was an audio version of a kind of scrapbooking technique which Lowe has adapted over the years.

> I really like that way of working. I kind of pretty much do that for every project. I will do a scrapbook type thing, where I just keep stuff that's inspired me, or images. I might go to a gallery to look at paintings or buy postcards of those paintings and rip out articles that have interested me and do little drawings and things like that. And it's all part of a kind of organic process, I think, that helps you think about things in a slightly different way. (Lowe, 2019)

Lowe also became involved with 'Ealing Live'. Essentially put together by a comedy development team at Ealing Studios, it was meant to be a kind of *Saturday Night Live* (1975-), only British, and it generally featured the kinds of up-and-comers who had already established themselves at the Edinburgh Fringe. As Lowe recalls:

It was people like Simon Farnaby Tom Meeten and Steve Oram and Gareth Tunnley, and people like Miranda Hart dipped in and out and Barunka O'Shaughnessy. And they [Ealing Live] asked us to come along and do a weekly show…and we want you to do new sketches every week, and just come up with new material every week, and we won't pay you, but we'll give you a rehearsal space and we'll give you a director. And at that time Paul King was directing these Ealing Lives. So, I think that's why I went along because he was involved and he'd directed *Garth Marenghi*. And I'd suddenly got this group of people – it was like *Carry On* shows or something – this group of people that were all going to work together, which is really unusual for comedy because you're quite a lone figure if you're a comedian. In a way, you're on your own. And suddenly there's this group of people, men and women, and that was quite unusual, there weren't that many women in comedy at that time. It was kind of Jenny Eclair and that was it, you know? Then, suddenly, we were all going to work with one another and all mix and match. So, me and Steve [Oram] said, shall we do a sketch about our parents really, Midlands figures. Then, as we started talking about it, these people became more and more sinister. And that was how *Sightseers* came about…
(Lowe, 2019)

Sightseers (2012), was directed by Ben Wheatley, one of the UK's most innovative and controversial filmmakers. He had already made kitchen sink thriller *Down Terrace* (2009), and the disturbingly violent *Kill List* (2011) and would later go on to direct the superb folk horror offering *A Field in England* (2013). His work is often seen as dark, edgy, honest, brutal and strange. The characters which populate his films seem somehow unable to fully engage with the rest of the world on any recognisable human level. Like Mike Leigh before him, Whealtey appears to want to exploit our very British sense of non-communication, and out of that quietness comes an unbearable unease which can often transform into random acts of extreme terror. And yet Wheatley's scripts, usually written or co-written by Amy Jump, are full of examples where misfit characters are forced together in overwhelmingly difficult circumstances, in essence being about the bonds which develop in moments of crisis. *Sightseers* would certainly fit that appraisal and the film would definitely, in terms of presentation and methodology, have his fingerprints all over it, but the bones of that project were developed much earlier in the hands of Steve Oram and Alice Lowe.

SIGHTSEERS

Image #4 – Poster for Sightseers *(2012) © StudioCanal/Film4*

Chris and Tina, the love-struck caravan obsessive protagonists at the heart of *Sightseers* began life as a stage act concocted by Lowe and Oram. Essentially, the two characters would discuss their mundane camping holiday adventures before slowly revealing to the audience that they were in fact serial killers. Seeing that the idea perhaps had legs and might make a solid basis for a feature film, the pair decided to make a short of the two characters which acted as a pitch to try and attract the attention of production companies. Though the clip began to create a buzz among industry types the idea was generally rejected for being too dark. Unperturbed, Lowe sent the clip to Edgar Wright whom she had worked with on *Hot Fuzz* (2007). Wright immediately saw potential for the project and passed it on to production company Big Talk, making himself executive producer and greenlighting the project.

Though the creation of Oram and Lowe, it was clear that *Sightseers* would inhabit the same universe which Wheatley had already begun to construct with his earlier films, as he states:

> I liked it because it kind of fit into my world view and it fit with *Down Terrace* and *Kill List* and I liked that they were thrill killers but didn't take a lot of thrill out of it and it was quite ordinary but they were extraordinary people and you got to see a lot of England, which you don't usually get to see, and I like the idea of the caravanning cos I like the, I like camping, I like caravanning, all that kind of stuff. So I wanted to do it in a way that wasn't taking the piss too much out of that. (Wheatley, 2012)

In fact, it fit so perfectly into Wheatley's vision that initially there was talk of including a brief cameo from Jay (Neil Maskell) and Gal (Michael Smiley) from *Kill List* into the finished production. It is clear, though, that the creative push and pull between Wheatley, Oram and Lowe was able to produce a disturbing, funny and original film incorporating love, death and English campsites. Perhaps partly channelling earlier American cult classics like *Badlands* (1973) or *The Honeymoon Killers* (1970), the film certainly plays around with the idea of the killer road trip, yet its presentation could not be more British and its most obvious influence would be Mike Leigh's TV play *Nuts in May* (1976). But what its interesting is how *Sightseers* takes some of those concepts from Leigh's play only to push them to their most violent and unhealthy extremes. In *Nuts in May*, the character of Keith (Roger Sloman) only appears to dance around the edges of actual GBH or worse: in one scene he threatens a fellow camper with a tree branch but he goes no further. *Sightseers*' character Chris, though, becomes a full-blown 'ginger-faced psychopath', using his own sense of righteousness as an excuse to mercilessly execute anyone who offends his sensibilities. The film also subverts some of the issues presented in *Nuts in May*. In Leigh's production the tension is mostly drawn from Keith and Candice-Marie's inability to communicate with anyone who doesn't fit within their barmy middle-class sub-structure. Keith in particular appears to go into meltdown when presented with the challenge of working-class revellers. In *Sightseers* though the inverse is often true: Chris, very working-class, feels most threatened by those he believes regard themselves as his social superior. In one scene, he batters in the head of a snarky ex-public school type: 'He's not a person, he's a *Daily Mail* reader.'

But essentially, *Sightseers* is a love story. The relationship which builds between Chris and Tina is palpable and feels real if a little odd. Again, it is Lowe's ability to emote both the absurdly horrific and the achingly humdrum in such a laughably believable manner that truly draws us in. This mundane form of weirdness can be seen in the 'Big Scribbler' giant pencil she uses to write home to her mother, or in the hand-knitted crotchless pants, or the baggy, ill-fitting jeans she slumps around in. In one scene, she attempts to seduce Chris in a restaurant by announcing she is wearing no knickers. When he not so subtly goes to have a look, and emerges from under the table declaring that he can't see anything, Tina then informs him that she is still wearing tights. It is her inability to grasp the unsexiness of her cack-handed seduction which makes her all the more charming and strangely dangerous. She is both frumpy and fascinating, a cagoule-wearing Rose West with a passion for murder, her man and Dolmio sauce.

Though the script was in place before filming began much of the dialogue we see on screen was born out of improvisation techniques. It was clearly a way of working that suited Oram, and particularly Lowe.

> Ben works in this really, really interesting way and it's one of the things which enables him to work really, really fast is that he dresses the whole set and lights it and then goes 'Now we can play the scene', and so actually we can go anywhere we want. So, it means as an actor it's much more like a piece of theatre, you can just walk in and do what you feel like you want to do rather than worrying whether you're hitting your mark or hitting your light or whatever (Lowe, 2012)

Fellow *Sightseers* actor and *A Field in England* star Richard Glover was also full of praise of Wheatley's style of operation.

> Ben is excellent and clever and really knows his stuff. He's pretty mellow on set, 'cos he's already got most of it planned out and visualised in his head. He kind of lets the actors do their thing. I heard him once saying he picks actors 'cos he trusts them, so therefore he lets them get on with it, and just occasionally gives gentle nudges or suggestions. Another cool thing he does is, sometimes he does a retake where he asks the actors to go slightly off script, improvise (but not too much), then the next take you go back on script, then off, then on, if you have the luxury of that many takes. This is a cool technique 'cos it helps you to say the words in a more natural, relaxed way when you're slightly improvising, and sometimes gives a more natural performance. (Glover, 2020)

Another unpredictably important character in *Sightseers* was the British weather. Filming everything on location and treating the shooting schedule as an actual caravanning tour of the English countryside, taking in places like Matlock, Mother Shipton's Cave, Holster slate mines and Lake Windermere, rain, sleet and howling winds all fed into the unfolding story. According to producer Claire Jones it was

> …a creative decision that whatever happened to us along the way we would incorporate it into the film, and I think that's really important when it comes to weather because you never know what to expect when it comes to England.
> (Jones, 2012)

Though this could make things slightly more uncomfortable for the crew and principal actors, it was a decision which elevates the reality of the situation, further stripping away any sense of Hollywood glamour from the death filled road trip in a distinctly no-frills thrill-killing package.

Tina's character arc is possibly the most interesting and revealing aspect of the film. Chris initially appears to be in charge of the relationship – he writes their holiday itinerary, decides the kind of break they will take and casually expects Tina to go along with his criminal activity when his homicidal tendencies have been exposed. Tina by comparison, at least at the beginning of the film, is mousy, quiet and hampered by her arrested development and a domineering mother. This seeming compliance is underlined at the beginning of their journey when she asks Chris to 'Show me your world'. Chris on the other hand asserts his manhood by taking control of the vehicle and telling Tina to pop travel sweets into his mouth at opportune moments by ordering her to 'mint me'. Tina's acquiescence with Chris's lifestyle is cemented in the aftermath of the first murder. She can easily back out of the whole sorry mess but instead decides to assert her willing collusion in his psychotic mission by echoing his earlier 'mint me' – it's a recognition that their geeky relationship runs darker and deeper than a mere a holiday romance. But whereas Chris seems drawn to his activities by a kind of madness, Tina becomes a slightly more dangerous prospect, taking to serial killing as easily as her other day-to-day activities. Like crocheting or knitting, killing becomes her unexpected new hobby: 'I've never thought about murdering innocent people before.' Like *Nuts in May* before it, the dynamic of the male and female protagonist is a shifting one. In Leigh's play, Candice-Marie (Alison Steadman) appears to be the more passive of the two. Keith is arrogant, controlling and domineering. However, as the story unfolds, Candice-Marie's stand point switches from passive to passive-aggressive and arguably it is Candice-Marie's badgering which really sends Keith over the edge. Similarly, in *Sightseers*, though Chris is ostensibly the one in charge, once his homicidal tendencies are revealed, Tina is able to exploit his madness to her own ends. It's a film about love and jealousy and like many of Ben Wheatley's projects it focuses on the bonds that develop between desperate and lonely people.

Tina's final defiance and hostile takeover of the relationship becomes clear at the climax of the story. After it is evident that the authorities are closing in on their activities – 'The police are pursuing a ginger-faced man and an angry woman' – the couple decide to commit a double suicide by throwing themselves from the top of the Ribblehead Viaduct. Yet when they count down to take their last leap into oblivion, Tina lets go of Chris's hand and she watches him plummet to his end while she looks down.

Though very much the product of a collaborative process between Lowe and Oram, which incorporated Wheatley's directorial vision, *Sightseers*, once explored more closely, seems to be the point where Lowe began to widen her creative milieu, at least more publicly, showcasing her talent not just for nuanced character acting but also her inarguable skills in terms of writing and development of ideas. Though the film received seven BIFA nominations, winning the award for Best Screenplay, and was largely praised by critics like Kim Newman who called it a 'uniquely British blend of excruciating comedy of embarrassment and outright grue', it didn't quite have the effect on the actor's career that one would have expected. As Lowe herself later stated:

> At that point, I had been in a kind of desperation about my career. I had written and starred in Sightseers, won some awards, then… nothing. And I think this is a common thing for actresses midway in their career. (Lowe, 2019)

But if that 'nothing' was an alarming prospect for a young actor, particularly one still eager to pay the bills on time, it could also be seen as an important incubation period, where a mix of desperation, determination and nothing to lose attitude, would eventually give birth to one of the most strikingly original British horror films. But what *is* the British horror film? What distances it from the scary movies of other cultures and how does this tiny island's world viewpoint, with all its camp, kitchen sink and comedic pedigree, still cast a spell on its inhabitants and those from around the world? And just how does *Prevenge* fit into this strange sub-sect of cinema?

Chapter 3: Island of Terror

> I am a total product of British film, horror, and of course comedy… I do think there's an inherent sensibility in Britishness that does not fear its own weirdness. And revels in its own low status…I don't choose it consciously, I don't think. It just comes out. But part of me indulges in the mundane and banal of all that, but also wants high drama and splashy event. And I like the mixture of those two things. And all of that, you mix it together and it has this punky anarchic texture to it, like 'fuck you, I'm gonna do it myself'. A bit scrappy, like Kathy Burke with a fag sitting on a wall. (Alice Lowe)

Whether it's Ealing's *Dead of Night* (1945), a Hammer or Amicus production, the folk weirdness of the early '70s staples such as *The Blood on Satan's Claw* (1971) and more recent chilling genre entries from the likes of Ben Wheatley, the British horror film has often existed in a unique, untranslatable place of its own. Homegrown offerings remain both a product of *and* commentary on the small rainy island they spring from, encapsulating stiff-upper-lip attitudes, class issues, rural heritage, folklore and dark pagan rumblings. They remain as nuanced and nationalised as South Korean shockers or Japanese J-Horror, yet many Anglicised productions doggedly refuse to be pigeon-holed into more easily definable labels such as the American slasher or Italian *giallo*. They are both annoyingly indefinable and delightfully elusive. Perhaps Reece Sheersmith, when discussing the appeal of Amicus films in the 2015 BBC Radio 4 documentary *The Houses of Horror*, comes close to describing the indescribable:

> When the smoke and the heaving bosoms and mist clear from the Hammer film you get the stark reality and grubbiness of the light on and an Amicus film and the pants on the floor. It is a little bit of a wake-up call to a version of horror that's kind of more unpalatable because it's more near the truth, there's something kind of raw about it all. (Shearsmith, 2015)

Prevenge clearly belongs to this world, bringing something new yet remaining a vital part of that history and tradition, which offers us the camp, horrific, quirky and sincere. But just what is British horror and what makes it tick? And how does *Prevenge* manage to encapsulate the essence of twentieth-century UK terror and also help modernise the form for the ongoing millennium?

If we put aside for one moment the contribution of Germany and its beautifully stylistic nightmares of the twenties such as *Der Golem* (1920), *The Cabinet of Doctor Caligari* (1920) and, of course, Murnau's iconic, unofficial *Dracula* adaptation, *Nosferatu* (1922), then one might agree that the horror film, at least the kind of horror film one knows and recognises, began in the burgeoning Hollywood of the early twentieth century. Spurred on by European directors, many of whom were seeking refuge from the Nazis, choosing to settle in the United States, American-produced horror films began to develop a life (or death) of their own. These movies, particularly the Universal films of the 1930s, though not always as sophisticated or visually distinctive as the earlier German Expressionist work, carried a gothic foreboding all of their own. As American as these features were, a handful of the best-looking and most subversive films from that decade, such as *Frankenstein* (1931), *The Old Dark House* (1932), *The Invisible Man* (1933) and *The Bride of Frankenstein* (1935), were in fact directed by someone who, like Alice Lowe, hailed from the West Midlands of England.

World War One veteran James Whale, a working-class gay man from Dudley, began his career as cartoonist before he switched his attention to the theatre. He directed a version of the RC Sheriff play *Journey's End* which transferred quickly to Broadway. The play proved so successful that it and Whale drew the attention of various movie producers. He initially signed a contract with Paramount but it would be his later work with Universal which would solidify his reputation. When his cinematic version of *Journey's End* (1930) did well at the box office, Karl Laemmle Jr, then head of the studio, offered him the choice of any project they had on their books. Whale chose *Frankenstein*, an adaptation of an eccentrically British piece of nineteenth-century literature. The film of 1931 followed on from the Tod Browning-directed smash *Dracula* from earlier that year. In comparison to Whale's finished product, the Bela Lugosi-starring Stoker reworking, aside from a few highly artistic flourishes and the title star's charismatic performance, was dull and stagey, its more obvious thrills dampened by seemingly endless parlour room conversations with a limply ineffective supporting cast of now forgotten also-rans. *Frankenstein*, though, with its genius casting of Boris Karloff (another Englishman) as the pathetically tragic man-made monster, coupled with Whale's keen eye for set design and graveyard sense of humour, presents us with a beautifully macabre classic modern horror. It not only provided Depression-era audiences with thrill-filled escape, it also touched upon the social concerns of the time, the ragged creature providing a handy metaphor for a battle worn, and now poverty-stricken population. As David J Skal suggests in *The Monster Show: A Cultural History of Horror*:

> Untold millions had been left with the feeling that modern life – and death – was nothing but an anonymous, crushing assembly line…Whale's film depicted a monster squarely in the grip of this confusion, a pathetic figure caught, as it were, between humanism and mechanism. (Skal, 1994, 135)

Of course, it was a huge hit, allowing Whale to produce a string of features which would prove to be increasingly more subversive than the last. Arguably, his masterpiece would be his final foray into the horror genre. *The Bride of Frankenstein*, was a gloriously camp and seductively wicked slice of black comedy, which managed to poke fun at organised religion and the marriage ceremony while lacing its imagery and dialogue with homosexual subtext and satirical wit, sidestepping the all-too-intrusive censorship of Joseph Breen and the austere Motion Picture Production Code. But, as British as these features were, with their eccentric Midlands-born director and largely English cast of players, they were technically American productions and it would be a few years before a more homegrown form of horror would erupt on the UK silver screen. But when it did it was lavish, gothic and bursting with Eastmancolor and Kensington gore.

Though other genre pieces had been made and released in UK including work like the Boris Karloff vehicle *The Ghoul* (1936), and 1945's excellent scary portmanteau effort *Dead of Night*, it would be Hammer Productions that would fully cement Britain's place in the horror firmament. As Sinclair McKay postulates in *A Thing of Unspeakable Horror*:

> In the midst of a febrile period in British culture and politics, stretching from the late 1950s to the mid-70s, when a sense of prosperity mingled with a feeling of seemingly unstoppable decline, it seems that Hammer films – bright, violent, titillating – were somehow calculated to insinuate their way into the murkier corners of the national unconscious. (McKay, 2007, 17)

Hammer would introduce the world to the likes of Peter Cushing and Christopher Lee and give star billing to future pin ups like Ingrid Pitt or Ursula Andress, and while the studio would create a whole range of products from thrillers to war movies, it would be their horror output that would most fully grab the public's attention. Taking their cue from earlier Universal pictures, Hammer quickly developed its own run of classic monster movies, reinvigorating old legends with a splash of colour and lashings of sex appeal. Spurred on by the success of Nigel Kneale adaptation *The Quatermass Xperiment* (1955), the company would unleash a run of now unforgettable midnight classics. Made largely within the confines of Bray Studios and following a strict, yet successful formula, directors like Terence Fisher and writers such as Jimmy Sangster were able to deliver not just entertaining and (for the time) daringly suggestive features but also create a recognisable imprint that would form, for many, an unshakable connection with their country of birth. Though Hammer as a company was an international success, it would be those born and raised in the UK who perhaps felt the greatest connection to those gory episodes of cinematic confection. Many, particularly those raised in this country in the '70s, will have felt a strong nostalgic bond to those James Bernard-scored gothic fantasies, and the classic horror double bills that would regularly form part of Saturday night TV viewing. The impact of Hammer horror on this country at the end of the fifties cannot be overestimated in terms of its success and cultural significance, in particular, the company's run of Frankenstein films, which not only took up where Universal left off, they, according to David Pirie, author of *A New Heritage of Horror*, considerably improved some of the weaker aspects. He describes Cushing and Hammer's take on the title role here:

> Rejecting the bland and self-pitying martyr of fate, whom Mary Shelley originally envisioned, Terence Fisher and his collaborators transformed the Baron into a magnificently arrogant rebel, in the direct Byronic tradition, who never relinquishes his explorations for one moment, even reviving the monster after it has been killed once, and conducting himself throughout with an utterly unscrupulous and authoritative elegance: he dresses with an extravagant attention to detail, enjoys food, wine and women, pursues studies in countless diverse fields and even sings softly in the laboratory as he works. (Pirie, 2008, 82)

And, of course, there was Lee's Dracula: if Lugosi had set pulses racing back in the '30s with his mysterious monochrome eastern European nobleman, then Lee, all burning eyes, blood and red silken cloak, became a terrifying yet irresistible demonic lothario, a vampire villain for the A-bomb generation. But it was not merely Hammer's big hitters that cemented the studio's legacy and created a legion of fans. It was often the slightly more off-kilter material and less-talked-about work like *Captain Cronos Vampire Hunter* (1974), *Rasputin the Mad Monk* (1966) or creepier B-movie efforts like *The Reptile* (1966) or *Plague of Zombies* (1966), that would create lasting, unshakable images that would both haunt and delight. The movies that would churn out of Bray studios alongside their lurid poster designs, often created long before a minute of film had been shot, somehow embedded themselves into the cold rainy landscape of the British psyche, springing from the same geographical place that bought us the romantic poets, and a gothic tradition. They were shaped between the chaotic years that gave us Harold Macmillan's 'You never had it so good' declaration, the Cold War and the 1978 'Winter of Discontent', and yet they were always, always an escape, an alternative to an early '60s UK film industry that would for a time be dominated by the angry young man and the 'social realism' of the kitchen sink drama. According to Sinclair MacKay:

> It is fairly clear that this frenetic frivolity was in itself a reaction to the grittiness of the late 1950s and early 60s productions – *Saturday Night and Sunday Morning* (1961), *This Sporting Life* (1963) and indeed anything else starring Racheal Roberts. Even Bryan Forbes's *Whistle Down the Wind* (1961) was relocated from the Home Counties to north… (McKay, 2007, 100)

Indeed, Dracula himself, or at least Christopher Lee, had some less than politically correct views on the matter:

> They should make films people want to see. Mind you, I haven't actually seen *Saturday Night and Sunday Morning* or *A Taste of Honey* but from what I hear about these so-called realistic films, the men are either thugs or queers and the women look like whores. If I want to know about the girl next door, I can knock on the door. If I want to be sick, I can go to hospital. (Lee, 1964)

But Hammer was not the only game in town when it came to British horror. Other studios would try their hand. Anglo Amalgamated's so-called 'Sadian Trilogy' encompassing *Horrors of the Black Museum* (1959), *Circus of Horrors* (1960) and Michael Powell's deeply disturbing yet sublime psycho-thriller *Peeping Tom* (1960), would provide a mixed bag of salacious delights to tempt away audiences from the staple of Hammer offerings. Later, Tigon would poach Lee and Cushing from Hammer and cast them in low-budget yet no less satisfying midnight scare fests such as *The Blood Beast Terror*

(1968) and *The Creeping Flesh* (1973). That same outfit would also release *Curse of the Crimson Altar* (1968), cult favourite *The Blood on Satan's Claw* and the Michael Reeves-directed *Witchfinder General* (1968) starring Vincent Price.

The late 1960s and early '70s saw the release of a seemingly endless run of successful and not-so-successful, distinctly British horror efforts. Slightly eccentric and occasionally totally barmy titles such as *The Abominable Doctor Phibes* (1971), *The Asphyx* (1973), *The Sorcerers* (1967), *Psychomania* (1973) and *The Wicker Man* (1973) fed into the collective nightmares of post-war, pre-Thatcher Gen-Xers, becoming regular staples of late-night telly. Perhaps Lowe's influences can be drawn most clearly from this era. We can find echoes of *Theatre of Blood* in Ruth's carefully orchestrated serial murders and there is something about her midnight sojourn onto the Halloween streets of Cardiff which channels the ghost of Ingrid Pitt. But there was really only one production company that could truly capture those English idiosyncrasies, kitchen sink outlooks and transpose them onto a raft of lunatic scary stories so completely effectively, and that company was Amicus. As Reece Shearsmith attests:

> I think an Amicus film is more real because suddenly it was things you hadn't seen, it was council estates, it was peoples' houses and it was on buses and it felt really close to home…it was the grisly 70s Britishness of them…(Shearsmith, 2015)

Oddly, though Amicus films became so synonymous with a British outlook, the company was founded by two Americans – producer Max J Rosenberg and producer/writer Milton Subotsky. But it's perhaps that level of 'foreignness' coupled with the fact that many stories developed for these films had their beginnings in the US, but were told via the grimy filter of dowdy low status viewpoints, that made them so special and grittily unique. As though these fabulous and exotic tales had to be re-written on old fish and chip wrappers for domestic consumption.

Though Amicus made other films, initially cashing in on the jazz/rock n roll craze with films like *It's Trad Dad* (1962), and would embrace TV adaptations like *Dr Who and the Daleks* (1965) and Doug McClure's rubber monster movies such as *At the Earth's Core* (1976), it was known primarily for its series of portmanteau titles from the mid-'60s onwards. *Dr Terror's House of Horrors* (1965), followed sharply by *Torture Garden* (1967) and *The House that Dripped Blood* (1971), very quickly developed the Amicus house style, that of the compendium feature. Taking its cue from the earlier *Dead of Night*, these portmanteau horrors would contain not one tale but four or five cobbled together by a linking narrative and shady, demonic host. For instance, in *Asylum* (1972), it is the manic orderly showing potential new doctors around the mental hospital; in *Tales from the Crypt* (1972), it is Ralph Richardson's creepy subterranean oracle; and in *From Beyond the Grave* (1974), it is Cushing's wonderfully charming curiosity shop owner ('I hope you enjoy snuffing it').

As time wore on and the portmanteau style features of Amicus continued, they seemed to become seedier and grainier, casting a somewhat darker shadow than the full colour gothic flourish of Hammer and the like. There were monsters in this world and the supernatural happened, but it was all viewed through the unwashed windows of an abandoned terrace house. This was where horror met with kitchen sink, ludicrous and terrifying, daft and depressing. One particular segment from Cushing vehicle *From Beyond the Grave* seems to typify the Amicus formula more than any other. In 'An Act of Kindness', the second story of the piece, we have tightly wound father Christopher Lowe, played by Ian Bannen, stuck in a dead-end middle-management job, mercilessly hen-pecked by a monstrous Diana Dors:

> Who do you think you're talking to in that tone of voice, some of the girls at your office? To them you might be the boss but I know what you really are, a jumped-up clerk, that's all an office manager is. Oh, it was different when we got married, you were a sergeant in the pay corp, soft job civilian future. Some future.

Lowe finds temporary reprieve from his hellish domestic set up when he chances upon street corner peddler and medalled ex-army lag, Jim Underwood (Donald Pleasence). Invited back to the street merchant's humble flat, Lowe develops a fascination for Underwood's creepily seductive daughter played by a quietly understated Angela Pleasence, Donald's real-life offspring. Of course, the story segment ends in a bloody mess of revenge, black magic and childhood wish fulfilment, but there is something so bare and squalid about that tale, that it strikes a rare nerve. It could only have been concocted in the dark mind of mid-'70s pop-culture, the decade that brought us power cuts and the 'Winter of Discontent', and imagined that the terrifying visions of *Pipkins*, *Bagpuss* and *Picture Box* were fit for pre-schoolers' televisual consumption.

Image #5 – Angela Pleasence in From Beyond the Grave *(1974) © Amicus Productions*

Though Amicus certainly ruled the roost when it came to the portmanteau horrors, it wasn't the only film company trying out the formula. World Film Services, which became Tyburn films, would later offer *Curse of the Werewolf* (1961) rip-off *Legend of the Werewolf* (1975), but would first release *Tales that Witness Madness* (1973). Although it was a patchier and admittedly much dafter version of the Amicus model, (a man passes over Joan Collins to make love to a tree trunk, etc.) it had a definite early '70s charm. In one memorable segment 'Penny Farthing', Peter McEnery is forced back in time via the antique bicycle of the title. The machinations are controlled by dead Uncle Albert, who initially appears to us in the form of photographic portrait which is terrifyingly able to change expressions depending on the situation.

A perhaps more established and better rival to Hammer and Amicus was the fairly short-lived (as least as a production company) Tigon. By the mid-'70s, it had effectively become a distributor for low-budget soft-porn titles such as *The Playbirds* (1978), *Sex with the Stars* (1980) and *Come Play with Me* (1977); but between 1967 and 1973 it produced a run of horrors that would implant themselves into the minds and nightmares of many a British youngster. Often mistaken for Amicus or Hammer productions, largely due its employment of Bray Studio stalwarts Lee and Cushing, its films were a heady mix of the deranged and the daft. *The Blood Beast Terror* brought us blood sucking were-moths, *The Sorcerers* an aging Karloff as mind control merchant, and in *The Creeping Flesh* an ancient skeleton brought back to life to wreak havoc on theories of evolution, not to mention Peter Cushing's sanity. But it would be the studio's foray into folk realms and beyond which would really cast a lasting shadow over the landscape of UK horror for years to come. Piers Haggard's *The Blood on Satan's Claw*, a somewhat nasty little tale set in rural eighteenth-century England, begins with the unearthing of an ancient skull, replete with still intact beady eyeball. It quickly descends into a grisly narrative of demonic possession, devil worship and ghastly goings on, its chills given an earthly reality by the use of on-location filming with its background of lush greens and rolling fields, nature providing a stark contrast to the deeply unnatural circumstances which arise. We can almost smell the damp soil, taste the dew on the grass as the blood soaks into the haystacks and another virginal teenager comes under the spell of a broody Beelzebub.

Whereas the supernatural was at the heart of *The Blood on Satan's Claw*, it was nowhere to be seen in earlier Tigon feature *Witchfinder General*, though it was talked about a great deal. This was a terrifically violent and obtrusively uncomfortable chronicle of seventeenth-century witchcraft trials. Matthew Hopkins (Vincent Price), the sadistic character of the title, might easily be a Trump, Johnson or Le Pen. A slightly more contemporary version of that kind of charming lunatic was used to make equally interesting points about US race relations in Roger Corman's excellent *The Intruder* (1962), starring a pre-*Star Trek* William Shatner.

Witchfinder General would not be the only, seemingly exploitative British horror movie to embrace social commentary in the 1970s. Criminally underseen *Death Line* AKA *Raw Meat* (1972), with its subterranean cannibal storyline which predated Tobe Hooper's much more talked about *The Texas Chain Saw Massacre* (1974) by a good two years, wasn't afraid to tackle 'meatier' subject matter. Interestingly both films focus on class and social status – while Leatherface and his family in Hooper's slasher might represent a beleaguered red-neck work force pushed to the edges of poverty and the limits of society, the underground flesh eaters of Gary Sherman's film might provide us with a handy metaphor for the dire consequences of capitalism and an unchecked establishment. Victims of the system, once used and abused are literally cast down to exist in a hell not of their making. The result is, of course, a re-criminative blood bath.

There would be no such message in Don Sharp's, incredibly entertaining but deliciously ludicrous *Psychomania* (1973). Dealing with a decidedly posh gang of motorcycle reprobates, who discover the secret of everlasting life (well, death), *Psychomania* revved 1973 up into not so much an *Easy Rider* (1969) style wave of rebellion but into a fit of giggles. A slightly confused Beryl Reid was at hand, so was a fairly stiff looking George Sanders (it would tragically be his final film). Arguably *Psychomania*'s ridiculousness and undoubted charms still resonate in the likes of *Garth Marenghi's Dark Place*, as its brand of cheap daftness and wrongly assumed confidence also seem to be at the core of Matt Holness's well-observed sitcom.

And while the British film industry would churn out horror movies throughout the 1980s, '90s and into the new century, it is perhaps that classic period of the late 1960s and early '70s which left the most obvious mark on the likes of Matt Holness, Ben Wheatley and of course Alice Lowe. It is not too difficult to pick out the hallmarks of classic British horror from Lowe's work, whether it be performance, writing or direction. And while she was soaking up other obvious influences via comedy and music, the signifiers of this particular brand of entertainment are clearly there.

Nicolas Roeg, specifically his seminal work *Don't Look Now* (1973), with its themes of bereavement and its dominant symbolic imagery, undoubtedly looms heavy over a film like *Prevenge*. Lowe may swap out the more mysterious setting of a wintry Venice for an autumnal Cardiff, replace gothic-style cathedrals and lonely ancient streets with pokey, cheap hotel rooms and gaudily lit subways, but Roeg's style and visual metaphors govern her directorial debut. The use of tunnels, small tight spaces opening out onto a wider world provide an excellent allegory for the pain of childbirth. Lowe also gives other nods to Roeg; the dreamlike 'otherness' of Ruth's world mirrors that of John (Donald Sutherland), lost between the planes of the living and the dead, while there is also the cheeky acknowledgement of the little girl's red coat in Ruth's scarlet Halloween death gear. Both films also share an unguarded sadness – these are deeply upsetting narratives about loss and desperation, each in some way being a twisted reflection of the other. Laura (Julie Christie) loses a child and struggles to make sense of the world alongside a husband she no longer fully connects to, while Ruth has lost a partner and is left carrying an unborn child she is hardly able to comprehend.

Prevenge might also share some DNA with several Amicus productions. Not only does the film mash together the supernatural with the ordinary, in a way that would have made Milton Subotsky proud, it can also be viewed as a portmanteau series of episodic chapters, echoing that studio's obsession with the anthology format. The 'linking narratives' of those films can be seen in the 'connective storytelling' elements of the midwife appointments featuring Lowe and Jo Hartley, which play out between the grisly goings on and more extreme moments. These set pieces act as a way to show us the inner workings of Ruth's conscience and the way she rationalises her own behaviour. Interestingly, although Ruth is at first completely resistant to the midwife's good intentions, responding in a defensive and obnoxious manner, she begins to soften as the birth gets closer, using the midwife sessions as a kind of confessional. This seems to be a direct mirror to the way she feels about the baby. In her initial meetings with the midwife, she becomes physically aggressive when she believes her unborn might be taken away by social services yet as the murderous narrative continues she grows ever more doubtful about the way she feels about her daughter, confiding that she would give her up in return for her old life.

And while *Prevenge* is at heart, a serial killer movie, it seems to have less in common with, for example, David Fincher's *Se7en* or *Zodiac* than it does with British period pieces like *The Abominable Doctor Phibes* (1971) or *Theatre of Blood* (1973) with their grand guignol, yet vaguely comic murder set pieces. After dispatching creepy reptile house keeper Zabek, Ruth turns her attention to DJ Dan, an unpleasant misogynist joke of a man, sweaty and fat in a ridiculous retro '70s afro. We as an audience spend more time with Dan than any of Ruth's other victims with the exception of Tom. It's a fascinating section of the story – although we have seen Ruth kill at the top of the film, it is here that we fully start to understand her motivations and modus operandi. We see her beforehand carefully choosing her outfit, having clearly done her homework; not only has she tracked him down to the pub where he is resident disc spinner, she has also studied what he is most likely to be drawn to. Playing up to his wants, and thinly veiled desires, she skilfully pulls him into her trap. It's one of the most darkly comic parts of the movie too. In one scene Ruth, quickly discards the alcoholic shot Dan has bought for her over her shoulder, and while this is unnoticed by him, the drink lands in the face of another innocent bystander who just happens to be behind her. In another, Dan, who has clearly had too much to drink, throws up into his wig in the taxi home, and to fully expose his repellent, utterly selfish way of being, Lowe has him lunge at Ruth, snogging her forcefully, vomit still dripping from his lips. Of course, Ruth has the last laugh, when she butchers his crotch with a carving knife. As he lays dying, she watches the blood spill from between his legs, in a mocking allusion to the pain of childbirth, and simply states 'It's messy, isn't it?'

But it is when Ruth takes out Len (Gemma Whelan) that we see her at her most cruelly playful. After bluffing her way into Len's house by pretending to be a charity worker, Ruth's actions don't go initially to plan. When her initial attack fails, Len is placed on high alert. Not only this, she is a fitness obsessive, so while Ruth struggles to comprehend what's happening, insisting that she's merely 'a working mother', Len dons boxing gloves and starts to punch her assailant in the face repeatedly. It is only when Ruth is accidentally jabbed in the stomach that Len feels a pang of guilt. In this second Ruth reacts quickly and without passion shoving the knife into her victim's midsection. Here, Ruth in full on antenatal mode, begins to tell the dying Len how to breathe in order to minimise the pain. But when the police sirens approach the house, Ruth is forced to make her escape through a dog flap, in another of the film's many visual birthing references.

This is not to say that Lowe doesn't also capture the grubbiness of other more serious British offerings. There is something in Ruth's dead-eyed motivation and the often cack-handed nature of her attacks which lends itself to the grim queasiness of Richard Fleischer's John Christie bio-pic *10 Rillington Place* (1971), the protagonist's quiet kitchen sink murder spree, in many ways as disturbing and unsettling as the actions of Richard Attenborough's softly spoken psychopath.

The lurid greens of the pet shop, the cold blues of the anonymous office building or the brightly lit underpass might mimic the colouration of *Don't Look Now*, or the Eastmancolor aesthetic of certain Hammer presentations, but it also incorporates other non-British influences. Ruth's late-night, heavily pregnant stroll through the subway tunnel harks back visually to Andrzej Żuławski's painfully overlooked *Possession*. When viewed again, Isabelle Adjani's miscarriage scene almost becomes a visual representation of Ruth's fractured state of mind. *Hellraiser* (1987), itself heavily influenced by *Possession*, with its perverse obsession with pain and ecstasy, also seems to shade some aspects of *Prevenge*. Clive Barker's splatter pic might have traded more liberally in the bloody manifestations of body horror, but the all-encompassing fear of actual physical transformation – an inconvenient pregnancy – are writ just as large in Lowe's story.

Yet, this is no cobbled together retrospective throwback, instead it conjures something new for the burgeoning century, avoiding the overly obsessive detailing and nostalgic romancing of The Love Witch (2016), a film from the same year. Prevenge understands its place within the framework of *modern horror*. And, like Lowe, who was part of a generation still sharing some of its existence with a post-war world, director Anna Biller acknowledges what has gone before but never ponders too long in a pre-constructed setting. This is a twenty-first-century film, though one that, like all good work, retains a certain timeless quality – it is a product of the now. Though Ruth daubs herself in Day of the Dead style make-up for Halloween, a ritual going back hundreds of years, the context feels new when coupled with the fact that she is a serial killer who is also heavily pregnant. The re-contextualising of older ideas so that they have a resonance with contemporary cinemagoers is expertly at play here. From Lowe's subversion of the slasher film to the inversion of clichéd views of motherhood, Prevenge, may recognise the undoubted influences of the 'old horror' but it is pointing its used butcher's knife clearly at today's audience.

But just how ready was that audience for the kind of horror film that would take our notions of what it is to be female, a mother or even human to its ultimate limits?

Chapter 4: Brat's Entertainment

Ted Post's low-budget exploitation piece *The Baby* (1973), is as alarming and charmless as its lurid original poster suggests. On it, the legs of an oversized man-baby hang out of a child's cot, the occupant's hand sticks through the bars of the crib holding an axe, while a scantily clad blonde in the background clings a teddy bear to her nether regions. The poster's text, perhaps undecided as to the film's strengths, opts for multiple taglines – 'Three, four, close the door', 'What goes on in the nursery isn't for kids' and 'There shall be mayhem wherever he goes'. This cultier-than-cult outing, brought to us by the same director that made *Beneath the Planet of the Apes* (1970), a follow-up to the original *Planet of the Apes* (1968), and arguably the best of the *Dirty Harry* sequels, *Magnum Force* (1973), is at times a sickeningly unpleasant wade through the quagmire of an uneasy psyche. It chooses to 'entertain' us with a story incorporating the domestic (and hinted at sexual) abuse of a man with learning difficulties, grisly murders, and, as Alex Cox once noted in his introduction to the film on BBC2's *Moviedrome*, it contains '…one of the most outstandingly sick endings of any film yet shown'.

It is not a film seen by the masses and those who *have* seen it tend to wear the experience as some sort of badge in one-up-manship. It is likely to inspire disgust in all but the most grimly determined horror buff and once seen it is difficult to un-see. However, what *The Baby* does do in all of its goo-goo, ga-ga madness is shift us away from our comfortable and well-established viewpoints on parenthood and, begins to explore a darker part of the equation, questioning the unconditional Hollywood spin on maternity and feminism. As Maitland McDonagh states:

> [It is] nutty yes, but also rooted in a very real fear that blossomed as the feminist movement encouraged women to reject the idea that happiness was marrying young, having babies, and keeping house for a faithful, hardworking husband. And *The Baby* is equally steeped in a visceral horror of children, little monsters of overwhelming primal neediness… (McDonagh, 2013)

Released the same year as William Friedkin's *The Exorcist*, another movie which sought to subvert more innocent depictions of childhood, *The Baby*, though an extreme example which largely flew under the radar, was certainly tapping into a darker cinematic conversation that was beginning to weigh heavy on the horror and sci-films of the '70s. A couple of years later we would have the British I Don't Want to be Born AKA *The Monster* (1975), a Joan Collins vehicle which according to its brilliantly pithy blurb was about '[A] little boy – born with what appears to be an innate hatred of people…'. And when we factor in a host of other films from that period, including *It's Alive* (1974), *The Omen*, *Who Can Kill a Child?* (1976) and *The Brood* (1979), and considering these outings were closely following the earlier *Rosemary's Baby* and *Village of the Damned*, it was clear that all was not well in the nursery.

When writing about *The Exorcist* in *Danse Macabre*, his excellent non-fiction book on horror, Stephen King perfectly sums up this growing anxiety:

> It is a film about explosive social change, a finely honed focusing point for the entire youth explosion that took place in the late sixties and early seventies. It was a movie for all those parents who felt, in a kind of agony and terror, that they were losing their children and could not understand why or how it was happening. (King, 1981, 196-197)

Alice Lowe's *Prevenge* is of course a key part of this continuing cinematic narrative. But how does it borrow, be influenced by or even transcend other filmic examples which pursue more visceral and disconcerting aspects of childhood, the mother and female empowerment?

Alien (1979), Ridley Scott's intergalactic haunted house movie about the attack on a small crew by a shapeshifting extra-terrestrial, was almost certainly heavily influenced by earlier pictures *The Thing from Another World* (1951), *It! The Terror from Beyond Space* (1958) and Mario Bava's *Planet of the Vampires* (1965). And it would have perhaps veered into even more familiar B-movie territory had the project been left with its creator Dan O'Bannon, who had pitched the initial idea as '*Jaws* in space'. However, after rewrites by producers David Giler and Walter Hill, Scott's production, especially when injected with the creative input of concept artists Jean 'Mobius' Giraud and the Swiss HR Giger, began to take on a more arthouse, European feel. The look of the piece, throwing the mining freighter Nostramo's grubby 'trucker' aspect against the twisted abomination of machine-meets-organic on the unknown planet, ensured that *Alien* left its audience with an unnervingly unforgettable catalogue of nightmarish visuals, seeding a sense of growing dread and misapprehension. But what it also did was develop into a strangely disconcerting examination of feminist – and anti-feminist – fears, concerns and uneasiness. This simple monster movie made with a largely male production team and cast, somehow morphed into a darkly lit allegory for the birthing process and, like *Prevenge*, it cut through the Hollywood maternity myth, presenting us with a more honest response pointing its shaking camera at the pain, blood and body distorting horrors of the female gestation process. As Barbara Creed states in *The Monstrous Feminine*:

> The primal scene is also crucial to *Alien* as is the figure of the mother, in the guise of the archaic mother. The archaic mother is the parthenogenetic mother, the mother as primordial abyss, the point of origin and of end. Although the archaic mother, the creature who laid the eggs, is never seen in *Alien*, her presence is signalled in a number of ways. She is there in the birth and death. She is there in the film's images of blood, darkness and death. She is also there in the chameleon figure of the alien, the monster as fetish-object of and for the archaic mother. (Creed, 1993, 17)

As with Lowe's film, *Alien* is littered with symbolic references to conception, birth and motherhood. The crew enter imposing womb-like tunnels via dark vagina-esque apertures, a parasitic creature erupts in violent caesarean fashion out of the body of a reluctant host; and phallic rows of teeth slide back and forth through the mucus-lined lips of the terrifying adult creature. The maternity theme is carried further with the introduction of 'Mother', the ship's computer guidance system; and when we are first introduced to the crew as they awaken from their cryogenic slumber, they crawl out of crib-style chambers wearing nappy-like underwear. Not only that, the film's poster campaign broadened those allusions with its stark uncomplicated imagery. As David J Skal notes in *The Monster Show: A Cultural History of Horror*:

> ...the crowning image of reproductive horror was yet to come. The poster art for *Alien* (1979) was deceptively simple and evocative: a cracked egg in a dark void, and the tag line *In Space, No One Can Hear You Scream*. Whether this was internal or external was not made clear. (Skal, 1994, 300)

Prevenge seems to mirror Scott's film in some aspects. Lowe certainly used the production as a reference point.

> ...films such as *Alien* are much more honest about motherhood in the sense of a 'hostile takeover'. It was important for me that, male or female, young or old, with or without kids, people identified with Ruth, that they were with her on her journey, they were seeing this through her eyes. I felt that if I could make the audience feel *like* Ruth, her sense of alienation, resentment, loss of control, that the film would have succeeded in its aim. (Lowe, 2019)

The idea of internal, real or imaginary body horror, or the 'corruption of self' which is explored in films like *Alien* and *Prevenge* is somewhat borne out by psychotherapist Jeremy Carne in his *Therapy Today* article 'Why does the Baby Hate Me?':

> A new parent may say they feel like an alien, only half recognisable as the person they were before, or that an alien has developed inside them. They may be afraid of harming the baby or themselves, or traumatised by the birth, overwhelmed by baby care responsibilities, panicky at the loss of self, drowned by sadness welling out of their own early experiences of neglect or abuse. (Carne, 2019)

Prevenge has other parallels with this earlier sci-fi classic, particularly its employment of a distinctly un-Hollywood female lead. Just as the character of Ruth strips away stereotypical representations of motherhood in the film's opening minutes, Ripley (Sigourney Weaver) also presents us with an atypical version of the 'final girl' trope, already established in horror movies like John Carpenter's *Halloween* (1978), or Tobe Hooper's *The Texas Chain Saw Massacre*. Ellen Ripley, in contrast to a host of female heroines that dominated the silver screen at the time, who in the hands of a patriarchal film industry could switch between handy victim or sex object, offered an altogether different representation of womanhood. Though a strong character she is also human, and Weaver resists turning her into the all-powerful and unrealistic domantrix super-girl of the young, and not so young, male fantasy. Ripley is calm, collected and cold, carrying out her duties to the letter of law. She is practical, resolute and seems to sit outside of the normal dynamics of the often-bickering crew. Her caring side is reserved not for her human companions but for Jonesy, the ship's cat. Jettisoned too are any hints of overtly sexual qualities, her drab faux-military fatigues offer no indication of titillation. One of the few concessions given to the male gaze comes at the end of the movie when Ripley strips out of her clothes to enter the cryogenic pod, mistakenly believing she has escaped the xenomorph. But for all of her strength she is also vulnerable to the kind of male oppression and matriarchal systems that many women face. The scene which most reflects this is perhaps the assault on Ripley at the hands of Ash, who though not human comes to represent a dominating and offensive male presence. Not only does Ash (Ian Holm) attempt to murder Ripley in a confined space adorned with naked female images, he does so by trying to choke her with a rolled-up pornographic magazine. The phallic 'weapon' he is forcing into her mouth creates a multi-layered symbolism reflecting the desire for some men to control women through means of sexual assault, enforced silence, or both. This kind of sleazy patriarchy is questioned in Lowe's film too; the character of DJ Dan is, though not physically violent, certainly the epitome of repulsive male aggression and sexism. An overweight, slobbering drunken pig, he meets his match when confronted by Ruth. Whereas Ash in *Alien* is decapitated, his head drowning in the secretions of sperm-like fluid, DJ Dan is robbed of his manliness and life, when his testicles are sliced off with a blade.

In another example, *Eraserhead* (1977), David Lynch's first feature film, released two years before *Alien*, we get an odd but slightly more autobiographical approach, in that it reflects the young director's anxiety concerning the imminent birth of his unexpected first child. And while he would not obviously experience the pain or unfolding physical change which his partner certainly would, it is clear these concerns were at the forefront of his febrile imagination during production. Now an undoubted cult classic, *Eraserhead* plays out like a monochrome fever dream. Henry (Jack Nance), the movie's off-kilter hero, with his explosion of toilet brush hair mimicking Elsa Lanchester's elaborate *Bride of Frankenstein* do, hobbles uncertainly through the stark industrial cityscapes of Lynch's nightmarish viewpoint. Black blood spills from still-moving roast chickens, pipes erupt through walls and ceilings and merge with the organic and unexplainable in a heady mix of impossible plumbing and steampunk sensibility.

When he becomes a father, Henry is driven mad with insomnia by the endless squawking of his strange, sickly offspring. The confines of his depressing apartment with its bricked-up windows and claustrophobic atmosphere create a horrific *mise-en-scène* walled with dread and frustration. And while Lowe, in *Prevenge*, leaves the demonization of the child to Ruth's slightly unreliable imagination, here Lynch explicitly shows us the 'reality' of Henry's miserable fatherhood. Not only is his child presented literally as a devilish and pathetic alien being, its limbless torso no more than a screeching, painful puppet, there are also numerous other symbolic references which underline the abject fears of becoming a parent. Behind a radiator is a deformed girl, who, during an unsettlingly out-of-context song and dance routine, stamps on sperm-like creations which rain from the ceiling. And, as Justus Nieland discusses in *David Lynch*, the dead plant and photograph of an atomic explosion by Henry's bed not only point to his now lifeless existence they also hint at his impotence; and how sex might be considered a destructive, not a creative force.

Lynch appears to carry through some of his concerns on this subject matter to his next film, *The Elephant Man* (1980). Focussing on real-life Victorian John Merrick (actually Joseph Merrick), a heavily deformed pauper forced to exhibit himself in freak shows to make a living, the director through use of a nightmarish opening sequence suggests that the abnormalities are kick-started in pregnancy when his mother is frightened by a marauding circus elephant. Though in actuality Merrick's considerable problems were caused by several debilitating bone conditions, Lynch cannot resist linking the idea of gestation with something unnatural and monstrous.

In 1976, Spanish director Narciso Ibinez Serrador was, in a kind of precursor to *Prevenge*, placing a heavily pregnant woman into a murderous narrative. *Who Can Kill a Child?*, made in the dying embers of the Franco regime, forces us, as with Lowe's film, to confront some difficult and none-too-digestible aspects of motherhood, childhood and parental self-preservation. When Tom (Lewis Fiander) and pregnant Evelyn (Prunella Ransome) take a holiday on a secluded Spanish island, hoping to rekindle a troubled marriage, they find themselves pitted against a gang of homicidal children. Though the reasons for the destructive behaviour are never fully explained, it is strongly hinted that the 'disease' is passed on by some kind of telepathy, à la *Village of the Damned*. In one sickeningly queasy moment, one of the murderous girls seemingly infects Evelyn's unborn child by placing a head and hand on her swollen stomach. When Evelyn is later killed by the infant within her, Tom is forced to take up arms against the ever-growing number of maniacal pre-pubescents, having to face up to his earlier crime, when he had tried to make Evelyn undergo an abortion. Though other 'monstrous child' stories had rolled out before, *Who Can Kill a Child?* stripped away the more obvious tangible aspects of child-demonization, which of course, makes the film's little terrorists an even more terrifying prospect. Unlike Linda Blair's possessed teen in *The Exorcist*, who exuded her inner demon mainly in the physical – her head spins around, she levitates, she spits green bile, etc. – these young villains appear unexceptional, their evil actions juxtaposed with smiles and sing-song voices. It is in this aspect that Serrador's production is most similar to *Prevenge*. Both films believably marry the ordinary and the extraordinary within the confines of a far from predictable horror narrative.

Canadian filmmaker David Cronenberg, who had already established himself as the body horror king with early low-budget productions *Shivers* (1975), *Rabid* (1977) and, of course, *Scanners* (1981) was able to weave in his own fear, paranoia and off-kilter worldview into his twisted cinematic visions, replete with diseased flesh and mental and physical deformity. His obsession with the 'infection' or parasite as dominant force, can easily be seen as a metaphor for the uncertain anatomical changes that come with pregnancy. Like *Prevenge* Cronenberg's movies don't insist on a moral stance; and often his antagonistic creations are presented, whether as insect monster or bloodsucking maggot, with their own perfectly reasonable desire to stay alive. Carrying a Lovecraftian feel, work from the first half of his career seems to revel in the outwardly grotesque; bodies change, skin pulsates, lives distort into gory ugly messes of sexual clinical fusion. In *The Fly* (1986), Seth Brundle (Jeff Goldblum), a scientist experimenting in matter transportation, accidentally merges his DNA with that of an insect. This kick-starts a rapid and somewhat cancerous transformation into the 'Brundlefly' creature. But it is during a nightmare sequence where Seth's estranged girlfriend Ronnie (Geena Davis) shockingly gives birth to a wriggling larva sack, that we are again taken back into those Lynchian-style apprehensions about procreation. Here sex is also seen as an act of destruction. But it is Cronenberg's earlier film, *The Brood*, a deeply personal piece that feels most connected to the themes present in *Prevenge*, with its focus of the monstrous child and unconventional motherhood.

Released the same year as *Alien*, *The Brood*, made in the reverberations of the director's messy divorce, details the story of Frank and his mentally disturbed wife Nola as they battle for custody of their only child, Candice. In a bizarre horror-show representation of his own experiences *The Brood* is both fantastical and semi-autobiographical. As Cronenberg states confidently, not to say somewhat resentfully:

> *The Brood* was certainly a very interesting and potent experience. It really was cathartically satisfying in a very direct way. Some of the violence in that movie was very cathartic for me to get on screen. Screaming and yelling. I don't usually have lots of screaming and yelling, but there's a fair amount of it in that movie. I don't do much screaming and yelling; I don't have it in my life. I don't like it much. But that was good stuff. It really worked. I certainly felt poised and in control during filming; it insisted on being made in a very personal way. It's as close to literal autobiography as I've ever come. I hope I don't come that close again. I can't tell you how satisfying the climax is. I wanted to strangle my ex-wife. (Cronenberg, 1992, 84)

The monstrous 'children' of the piece, spawned asexually from the exterior womb of 'mother-creature' Nola, are products of a disquieted mind. Tufts of blonde hair top deformed and distorted faces, their dwarf-like bodies are clothed in blood-spattered romper suits and they pursue their murderous actions quickly and mercilessly, as mutated cousins to Wyndham's *The Midwich Cuckoos*. Like *Prevenge*, the film also hints at the daunting pressures of motherhood which can materialise as mental health issues, be they temporary or permanent. Nola, like Ruth, is a raging and uncompromising maternal brand of chaos.

'Nature's a bit of a cunt though, don't you think?' says Ruth to her slightly befuddled mid-wife (Jo Hartley). There are several of these scenes throughout *Prevenge*, created as two-handers like most of Ruth's encounters. They also act as a centre point, a kind of palate-cleansing buffer between the blood-fuelled bedlam which dominates much of the story. It is here we sail closest to Ruth's 'reality', where we are reminded more solidly that her experience is (even without the added complication of serial murder) a difficult, scary and complex one. Pregnancy, though hardly an unusual occurrence, can become a very un-normal experience. The midwife's initial inability to connect with Ruth on any level other than with cold superficial professionalism highlights the protagonist's distance from the rest of the world. Although the murder scenes are visceral and violent, laced with humour and a satirical edge, we arguably feel Ruth's anger and frustration most acutely during these more intimate clinical moments. Conversely, Ruth's odd relationship with her dominating unborn daughter underlines her own 'loss of self' and demonstrates just how far she has been cast adrift from everyday living. The illustrations in her diary, (actually written and drawn by Lowe) burst with marker pen wrath and personal outrage. One image in the book depicts Ruth as some kind of mythical figure incorporating strong female characters from fiction and reality. Her hair is alive, a mockery of Medusa snakes, she wields a knife above her head in Boudicca-like pose and the child inside her is exposed in X-ray fashion. We see inside her belly, again making us face the body horror implications of pregnancy, but the image also gives us more of a glimpse inside Ruth's mind. It also highlights the contradictory quality of Ruth's existence. She is both creator and destroyer of life. The midwife tells Ruth that she has a 'force of nature inside her' and that 'baby knows best, baby knows what to do', yet her fractured viewpoint also seems to tell her (via the illusion of a cognisant foetus) to kill and seek revenge. According to Lowe, this ongoing 'diary' element of the film, was born out of the need to present Ruth as classic serial killer, with a downtrodden twist:

> …Serial killers usually have pictures on a wall don't they? They have like a collage. Photos of the victims, weird torn out newspaper cuttings. But I was like well, she [Ruth] doesn't really live anywhere, she doesn't have that, but what's the equivalent? And it was going to be this book. And I thought well, I'd should really start doing this book as I don't think anyone else is really going to understand what I really want it to be, so, I'll just have to do it myself. So, I bought a baby book in Paperchase and I started setting out defacing it, and I remember I was on the train, and I'd started defacing it with weird drawings, and this woman, who had been sort of looking at me looking at me thinking 'Aw you're pregnant, that's sweet' was giving me this look now of 'Oh my God, you're demented'. So, I put it in the film. (Lowe, 2019)

In a cinematic and in a clearly much more exaggerated sense, *Prevenge* highlights the disconcerting mood swings and changes which accompany some pregnancies. Ruth is psychotic, a killer, a mother, but more importantly she is still a woman. And while Lowe refuses to take the more well-trodden path to create a clichéd tale of sisterhood, she is equally not afraid to show Ruth's less callous side. After the character has dispatched DJ Dan, Ruth takes out time in her busy schedule of slaughter to see to the elderly, senile mother of her victim, putting her to bed and washing the dishes. This also encapsulates Lowe's custom brand of wit and horror, the splicing together of the outlandish with the domestic. This 'compassion' rears itself in other ways too; as she is about to execute Tom, she is suddenly thrown into a fit of guilt when confronted with the swollen belly of his pregnant partner. This state of duality of being torn between what 'her baby' is telling her to do and what other, more rational voices are saying, such as her midwife's refrain of 'You have to decide what's right and what's wrong', is represented visually by the repeated mirror images we see during the Halloween night scenes. Other indications of Ruth's confused state are symbolised in a scene which seamlessly juxtaposes her willingness to fit in and be a 'proper' mother with her continued desire for bloody revenge. In it, we see Ruth attending an antenatal yoga class; however, this is intercut with doom-laden shots of her wandering mournfully through a graveyard. It's a perfect filmic manifestation of her potential to be both life-giver and a life-taker.

The presentation of Ruth as Travis Bickle-esque anti-hero, devoid of the more commonplace tropes we expect to see in other cinematic versions of the expectant mother, places *Prevenge* and its protagonist into rarely explored territory. What gives Lowe's film more depth is the way in which she is able to offer us a brutally simple and yet strikingly complex individual, who never asks for our sympathy but somehow (almost) gets it. Ruth may be, on the surface, a revenge-hungry psychotic but it is the fact that she is also so genuinely broken that garners our interest. Again, is there anything so truly upsetting as hearing Ruth say to the midwife that she would give up her unborn child to get her boyfriend back? The harsh yet believable essence is borne out of research Lowe undertook on real-life cases where pregnant women had lost their significant others in tragic circumstances.

Not only does *Prevenge* subvert our expectations when it comes to the representation of motherhood and present us with a less-than-conventional main character, it also forces us to second guess its more feminist agenda. Lowe's production can certainly be seen as 'a feminist piece' for want of a more nuanced term; there are countless occasions where the story points us to the gender inequalities inherent within our culture. Yet it also refuses to be too bogged down in more obvious left-wing rhetoric. Like the Maxine Peake vehicle *Funny Cow* (2017), it is a film which is undoubtedly feminist in its outlook but it is also raw and messy, steadfastly denying any hint of middle-class niceness to creep in (both films coincidentally use red as a visual signifier). This is womanhood in all its bloody, non-polished reality. Interestingly two of Ruth's more memorable killings take out female characters, dispatching perceptions that this film is simply a violent battle of the sexes affair. Ruth's first female victim is Ella, a hard-nosed, yet outwardly polite HR type, completely at odds with Ruth's pregnant predicament.

Like the worst example of a male chauvinist, she is unable to see past her interviewees' current state. Ruth, as a pregnant woman, is reduced to a thing, a lengthy maternity break or a child dependent liability. Ella's obtuse attitude in some ways feels like an actual betrayal, rather than the fully expected idiocy of a character like DJ Dan. Later victim Len is dispatched in a more comic fashion, yet the image/fitness obsessed character can be viewed as a convenient and literal punchbag, symbolising Ruth's (or possibly Lowe's) frustration with male perceptions of the perfect body.

There is also something about Ruth's method which seems to hark back to more archaic male viewpoints on birth, pregenancy and the womb. The ancient Egyptians and Greeks, as noted by Lisa Appignanesi in her book *Mad, Bad and Sad: A History of Women and the Mind Doctors from 1800 to the Present*, believed that

> ...the womb or uterus was a free-floating entity which could leave its moorings when a woman was dissatisfied, to travel around the body and disrupt everything in its passage, hysteria was thought to be able to produce any number of symptoms, both physical and mental. (Appignanesi, 2008, 162)

Even in the nineteenth century, it was a widely-held belief with many medical professionals that forms of female 'madness' were linked physically to the uterus. The words hysteria and hysterectomy are derived from the same origins and as Appignanesi goes on to say:

> It worth noting that in Britain, throughout the [nineteenth] century, medical believers in the popular reflex theory, which found correspondences along the lines of the nerves between body parts were rather less neutral in their observations and liked to trace mental symptoms back to women's reproductive system. They were quicker to stigmatise all women as 'more vulnerable to insanity' than men because the instability of their reproductive systems interfered with their sexual, emotional, and rational control. (Appignanesi, 2008, 91)

Lowe, as Ruth, seems to berate these antiquated and ridiculous notions, as well as their modern-day equivalents that exist in a carefully constructed gender-biased society, twisting them into a bizarre fantasy where male-led aspects of restriction are shaped into a nightmarish weapon. When her womb literally comes to life and her unborn child strives to drive her mad, she becomes not the locked away victim of a Victorian asylum but a destructive force on a hellish rampage. Those old lies have come back to haunt the patriarchy and all it stands for. *Prevenge* becomes a fierce mockery of the outdated and still rampant sexism that abounds in this deeply unequal system.

Like *Rosemary's Baby* before it, *Prevenge* contains murder, mayhem and a devilish child and yet neither film is about the fear of death. Like its predecessor Lowe's film works because is about our concerns with modern living. Unlike Polanski's film however, it is not afraid to take a more forceful step, willing us to ask the question, what happens when our loved one dies and we don't?

Chapter 5: Mourning Gory

One of the breakout chillers of 2018 was Ari Aster's debut feature *Hereditary*. Starring Toni Collete and centering on a family unhinged by witchcraft and unearthly occurrences, its bombastic, no-holds-barred visual style left an undeniable mark on the minds of cinema goers. But it was also an excruciatingly painful look at guilt, breakdown and bereavement. Collete's turn as broken matriarch Annie, dragged into an increasingly bizarre supernatural world of evil in the wake of her mother's funeral and death of her youngest child, is both heart-breaking and unbearable. Collete was in fact a formative influence on the young Alice Lowe, who had been transfixed by her lead role in Aussie coming of age comedy, *Muriel's Wedding* (1994).

Though *Hereditary* explodes into a full-on horror film climax, much of the production can be seen as a twisted metaphor for Annie's state of mind. She and her immediate family literally and figuratively lose their heads, rather than face up to the certainty of death. Characters project their grief (or lack of it) in different ways, creating realities of their own making. Annie, a freelance artist, meticulously constructs miniature recreations of some of the most painful episodes in her life; indeed, the film is shot in a way that often makes the audience question whether they are witnessing 'reality' or an intricately modelled version. Members of the family also fail to cope in other ways. Peter (Alex Wolff), the son, loses himself in a world of social media and marijuana while Charlie (Milly Shapiro), the daughter, invents distorted versions of the world around her via disturbing puppet fabrications pieced together with trash and the remains of dead animals. It's an uneasy watch at times and its bloody, hopelessly grim finale nudges it, at least visually, towards the arena of the exploitation film, yet at its core this is an unflinching examination of relationships, familial or other, and how they can be decimated or strengthened by bereavement.

Our inability as a species to reflect sensibly on our own mortality pervades not just *Hereditary* but a host of twenty-first-century horror movies. Many female characters in recent genre pieces are placed in a dreamlike netherworld, caught halfway of between the now and a haunting past. This can be seen just as clearly in Aster's follow-up, *Midsommar* (2019), another film with a plot powered by grief (the protagonist's family has been wiped out in a bizarre suicide/murder pact). The triumphant smile on Dani's face (Florence Pugh), after her cheating boyfriend has been horribly dealt with at the film's end, seems to mirror Ruth's manic act of defiance at the end of *Prevenge*.

Ruth in *Prevenge* is both bringer of death and victim of cruel bereavement. As Lowe discusses, the passing of Ruth's significant other is shaped into the symbolic representation of being robbed of one's own character during those expectant months.

> I think maybe it's because we're really not used to the idea of women having existential crises. Like, 'who does she think she is, having a meltdown over nothing?' – Greta Thunberg [*laughs*]. Whereas if Hamlet does it, or the Joker (Joaquin Phoenix's), or Travis Bickle, or WHOEVER, it's absolutely fine, completely understandable. Although Hamlet was also grieving, but, you know, as a symbol of angsty navel gazing, there are few female parallels. (Lowe, 2019)

Lowe's theories are borne out, especially when we examine other modern work such as *The Babadook* (2014). Written and directed by Jennifer Kent, this simple but terrifying look at single parenthood in the aftershock of sudden death, creeps unnervingly at first and grows into a fully blown dark night of the soul. At times bleak, the film is a spiralling account of Amelia (Essie Davis), a beleaguered woman's exhausted plunge into a continuing trauma, made worse by a seemingly uncaring outside world and her 'difficult' son's frustrating behaviour. Like *Prevenge*, *The Babadook* casts aside our cosy perceptions of the mother/child set up. Samuel (Noah Wiseman), Amelia's six-year-old, is not the supportive and loveable offspring we are treated to in other, less inspired work. In Kent's handling, he is shaped into an uncontrollable Tasmanian Devil-type handful, dangerous and incapable of existing without constant attention. As Kent stated at the time:

> I'm not a parent but I'm surrounded by friends and family who are, and I see it from the outside…how parenting seems hard and never-ending. I thought the film was going to get a lot of flak for Amelia's obvious shortcomings as a mother, but oddly, I think it's given a lot of women a sense of reassurance to see a real human being up there. We don't get to see characters like her that often. (Kent, 2014)

We see Amelia reduced to a mental health wreck, bought to her knees by Samuel's constant demands and the onslaught of work, lack of sleep and the continuing disruption of the pervasive Mr Babadook, itself a cruel metaphor for her inability to move on after bereavement. The devastating sense of being sucked into an abyss is incredibly acute; one cannot help but feel for Amelia, even though at times she can't stand the sight of her challenging child, and her motivation leans towards the neglectful. Her eyes, no more than dead pools of regret swirl in the horrifying realisation that at least for now, this is her all-consuming everything.

It rams home the message that parenthood, especially single parenthood, can for some be a literal waking nightmare and that the accepted view of 'unconditional motherly care' no matter what happens, is ever so slightly erroneous. It is *that* truth that society seems incapable of addressing, which makes films like *The Babadook* and *Prevenge*, both refreshing and jarring. Yet Lowe, now a mother of two, is also at pains not to suggest that individual children are the cause of extreme forms of negative behaviour:

> For me, it was the perfect way to let Ruth off the leash, to disconnect her from relationships and society. Something's been cut short, unnaturally. And this tips her into anarchy. The subtext is that Ruth's relationship with the father of her child is extremely ambiguous. We don't know if he loved her, wanted the baby, was even with her. I think she was almost certainly mad before, and the relationship loss has triggered the killings. At the end of the day, the madness comes from her and not the baby (which is revealed at the end). This idea that having a baby does not change you. For better or worse. You are just who you are. Plus a baby. (Lowe, 2019)

One of the most eloquently successful British horror films to explore the nature of relationships, grief, parenthood and guilt, is the previously discussed *Don't Look Now*. But Roeg's fractured presentation of reality is perhaps never more apparent than in work like *Performance* (1970), *Walkabout* (1971) and *The Man Who Fell to Earth*. As with Prevenge, two of these productions deal with characters surviving in the wake of a family bereavement. In *The Man Who Fell to Earth*, David Bowie's alien struggles to continue on earth without his family. While it is hinted that they have already perished on his drought-plagued home planet, he drowns himself in alcohol. In *Walkabout*, a teenage girl (Jenny Agutter) is forced to look after her much younger brother in one of the harshest environments on Earth in the wake of her father's suicide in the Australian Outback. But *Performance* also deals with another subject linked to Lowe's film, that of individuals facing that complete 'loss of self'. Steve Rose of *The Guardian* described

Roeg's cinematic offerings thus.

> [His films seem] to shatter reality into a thousand pieces [and are] unpredictable, fascinating, cryptic and liable to leave you wondering what the hell just happened… (Rose, 2008)

Don't Look Now, though, focuses on married couple John (Donald Sutherland) and Laura (Julie Christie), currently residing and working in a gloomy off-season Venice, after the tragic death of their youngest child. Haunted both physically and metaphorically, the story, a typically puzzling Roeg production replete with shifts in time and a patchwork narrative, plays out like a dizzyingly hypnotic dance. Its muted colours, bar the vivid red of a dead child's coat, enhance the dowdy nature of the day-to-day lives of the central couple. The film's famous copulation scene is memorable because it is so matter of fact and so deliberately 'un-sexy'. John and Laura are embroiled in a supernatural game of cat and mouse when introduced to oddball blind psychic Heather (Hilary Mason) and her sister Wendy (Clelia Matania), and it becomes apparent that the horror of their situation is entwined in a string of brutal murders. But this is a different kind of British horror to the one established by the likes of Hammer. So fragmented is the storyline that we, as an audience, often forget where we are at in space and time. Yet it is its grim sense of ordinariness that most pervades, never more so than in the film's horrific opening sequence. In it we watch a seemingly happy couple with two children have their lives utterly destroyed in a few seconds. A red coat, a lake and two horrified parents replace the usual velvet cape, castle and fangs in a new kind of stomach-kicking dreadfulness. But what is most palpable about *Don't Look Now* is its utterly real sense of devastation. The grief is all too apparent. And like *Prevenge*, that sense of loss is never quite displayed in the way we are expecting. One of the most interesting elements of the production is the way that John and Laura appear to abandon their one remaining living child, who is left in a boarding school back in England. Roeg flouts our natural assumptions about death drawing families closer together, for a story about the irrationality of bereavement. Both John and Laura, though physically together, seem to exist in separate worlds. Laura clings to an afterlife fantasy while John throws himself into his work. Interestingly, John's restoration of churches, given his clearly rationalist leanings, seems to be a tragic indication of his need to build a more acceptable veneer around himself in an effort to mask his quickly consuming darkness.

As usual, much of Roeg's presentation is discovered in the editing process, a method of storytelling advocated by Lowe herself:

> I worship at the altar of Nic Roeg, et cetera. My belief is that the power of filmmaking is enough. The tools for creating whatever dreamscape you want are already there, and were already established long ago, '60s, '70s, earlier even. You can depict a mental breakdown, an alien world, a psychic state, with just editing, music, sound and theatre. You don't need a whole bag of CGI. Some of this comes from a habit of low budget constraints. But generally, I do prefer it. So, a lot of my stuff probably is unconsciously retro, whilst the stories I want to tell are probably more about modern anxieties/preoccupations. (Lowe, 2019)

Other than Roeg's visual flair, which Lowe incorporates with particularly reference to *Don't Look Now*, with its use of red as a key colour and its grittier *mise-en-scène*, what both films truly have in common is the completely believable and demoralising sense of anguish experienced by protagonists Laura and Ruth. Though both of these characters are very different people, what they share is a broken perception of reality and how they adjust their experiences to suit this unwelcome new normality. Laura chooses to channel her bereavement into the unlikely belief that her daughter now exists in a post-life world of spirits and ghosts. Ruth, though, is so completely lost without her late partner that she forgoes any conventional motherly link between herself and her unborn daughter, instead choosing to live in a fantasy where her child becomes the key motivator in her life of murder and revenge. Her refusal to accept what society expects of her is highlighted in an angry exchange with Tom: 'I'm not grieving, I'm gestating.'

Conversely, Roman Polanski's earlier *Rosemary's Baby* deals with grief of a different kind. Young Rosemary (Mia Farrow) is presented with a series of losses. First, she loses her more familiar grounding when she and husband Guy (John Cassavettes) move to a swanky new apartment. She also loses her privacy and feeling of independence when her everyday existence is blighted by the busybody intrusiveness of overbearing neighbour Minnie (Ruth Gordon). She then loses her freedom when she is hampered by pregnancy, her life partner when the truth about Guy is revealed, and finally, in light of the horrible reality presented to her, she arguably loses her sanity. Yet the key difference between Ruth and Rosemary is the latter's embrace of expectant motherhood and the former's seeming reluctance. Even when faced with rearing the actual son of the Devil, Rosemary's maternal instinct strengthens. In Lowe's film any semblance of a mother-daughter bond is fractured into a thousand murderous pieces. In many ways, this is why *Prevenge* transcends many other British or American slasher movies. Ruth is a much more complicated persona than we are used to experiencing within the confines of what many perceive as a more throwaway sub-genre.

Another more complex view of motherhood and loss is also presented in Babak Anvari's Iranian ghost film, *Under the Shadow* (2016). When Shideh (Narges Rashidi) decides to stay in the heavily attacked Tehran during the Iran/Iraq war, she is forced to look after her daughter in increasingly difficult circumstances. Not only does she face the physical reality of bombs falling from the sky, there is also the more existential (yet equally) terrifying threat of unseen supernatural beings. The tension is drawn not only from the obvious fear that the protagonist and her daughter feel towards these opposing forces but also from the uneasy relationship that builds between them. Far from exhibiting the kind of unconditional care one expects to see, Shideh presents a more complicated take on motherly love; though she clearly does her best to offer protection, it seems to be protection which is born out of a duty thrust upon her. Suffering the temporary loss of her husband, who has been called up to military service, and the permanent loss of her own medical career in the wake of the Iranian cultural revolution, Shideh has been shanghaied into the life of domestic homemaker. Not only that, Iran's strict dress code and after hours curfew make it increasingly difficult for her be the person she desperately needs to be. The barely concealed anger about her own enforced role of housewife and carer bubble to the surface, her bitterness exhibited in the short shrift she extols on her, at times, trying young child. *Under the Shadow*, though very much a film in its own rights, shares much in common with *The Babadook*, both films dealing admirably with more nuanced depictions of more difficult single-parent set ups – one depicts a mother caught in the midst of an actual war, the other deals with a mother's battle for her own sanity.

Prevenge, though, like *Under the Shadow* and especially *Don't Look Now* presents us with something capable of being both fantastic and dauntingly real. Roeg never allows us to escape John's grim fate, particularly when faced with a female murder victim being pulled unceremoniously from the freezing Venetian canal, her skirt hanging down revealing filthy tights and underwear, but he also creates a heightened sense of suggested fantasy, his flashes between past, present and future creating an unearthly and disconcerting illusion where ghosts, heaven and hell co-exist. Lowe in some ways plays the same trick. Ruth's actions appear to take place within a recognisable normality of pubs, flats, hotel rooms and Halloween parties, but she also seems to exist outside of the ordinary limitations of real life. Although she is not the most adept murderess, the bodies she leaves in her wake are never investigated. As far as we know, no links to these crimes are seemingly ever signposted, aside from in one scene when we hear an approaching police siren. As Lowe states:

> I come back to this time and time again, even when I'm writing. It's about polar opposites often, the thing that makes something interesting. It's like cooking a meal, it's like ooh this is a bit too earthy, we need to put something lemony in it to make it sharp, you know? It's like often in the edit of a film I'm like, this is too schmaltzy, it needs to be harder now. We've gotta have that in the mix, and I think it is…it's about having that right balance of stuff that you kind of go 'oh, I thought it was going too far that way but it came back and got pulled back the other way'…It's about not being generic…its doing something and putting a twist on it that makes it its own thing. (Lowe, 2019)

Making a film 'its own thing' can often be about taking risks or having the conviction in an idea. It can also be about recognising fairly early on when an element of a project is not working. Part of *Prevenge*'s effectiveness is born out of its simplicity and avoidance of more convoluted storytelling. This simplification or streamlining led to a more complex sub-plot being axed from the production. According to Lowe:

> There was mother-in-law character, which was like the mother of the father of her child, who'd kind of been intimating that she's going to take the baby from her if she [Ruth] doesn't form a kind of relationship with her, kind of thing. But again, it just wasn't…you have this kind of, there's a kind of purity about those characters being in their own bubble. Sort of untethered from the rest of the world, which is true in *Prevenge* and *Sightseers*, that there's some sort of suspension of disbelief, makes them almost a bit like children or something, that they're like Peter Pan, they're just cut off from reality a little bit. (Lowe, 2020)

This distancing of characters from reality can obviously be mishandled; too little distancing and an audience won't care and too much and it may not follow or believe a particular story. Fortunately, there have been several noteworthy examples where disturbed female characters have been 'distanced' from reality to great artistic effect. This disassociation is mentioned by Kier La Janisse in her autobiographical/historical film text, *House of Psychotic Women*, in the wake of a difficult childhood trauma.

> I started to disassociate from an early age; I would often imagine that I was one of those changeling children I read about in fairy stories, a substitute for a real child that had been stolen away because it was more perfect. (Lowe, 2020)

This disassociation of a damaged character from reality is illustrated in Polanski's pre-*Rosemary's Baby* psychological thriller, *Repulsion* (1965). Socially awkward Carol (Catherine Deneuve), when left home alone by her sister, descends into madness. The hinted childhood abuse rises to the surface and the fractured protagonist finds herself at the mercy of evil rapist landlords and a home space which takes on a demented nightmarish sentient quality of rotting rabbit flesh and nightmarish arms protruding from the shadowy walls. As Kier La Janisse continues in *House of Psychotic Women*:

> From today's perspective *Repulsion* is a virtual catalogue of the tell-tale trappings of the 'neurotic woman' horror film – the insular plot, the dis-integrated characterisation, stylistic flourishes such as repeated mirror shots, disembodied hands that grope the protagonist, the actual or optical enlargements of sets to create disorientation, the low-angle shots of the woman swiping maniacally at her victim – but *Repulsion* is perhaps grandmother of them all. (Janisse, 2012, 310)

Repulsion is part of Polanski's so-called 'Apartment Trilogy' comprising this, *Rosemary's Baby* and finally the often overlooked *The Tenant* (1976). Each building featured in the separate films might be seen as a reflection of the state of mind that their protagonist inhabitants find themselves in. In *The Tenant*, the small living space equates to an increasingly more hostile environment towards foreigners or outsiders. Trelkovsky (Roman Polanski himself), an immigrant, finds his tiny world dominated by small-minded, xenophobic neighbours. The lavish apartment in *Rosemary's Baby*, blank and empty at first before gradually filling with possessions and interfering strangers, could also be viewed as a handy metaphor for Rosemary's womb and reflect the difficulty of coping with a fairly terrifying pregnancy and her erstwhile 'bodily invasion'. But it is the black and white flat of *Repulsion* which most clearly taps into a disturbed character's mindset. Carol's 'otherworldliness' also echoes the earlier *Carnival of Souls* (1962). Heck Harvey's highly influential (yet largely unknown outside of cult horror circles) film, is a strange, ethereal and dreamlike drama. Its woozy action drifts from the all-too-real locales of grotty bed sitting rooms with creepy housemates to the phantom dance parades of abandoned ghost world holiday resorts. Protagonist Mary (Candace Hilligoss), who is involved in a car accident at the beginning of the story recuperates and decides to make a new life for herself in a different town. But 'life' is the last thing she finds. Haunted by a ghoulish figure known only as The Man (Heck Harvey), her existence subsides into a grim unreality of illusions and paranoia until the 'truth' of her situation is bought tragically home. Mary's own loss arrives when she gains an insight into who she really is — a newly assigned recruit of the walking dead. *Jacob's Ladder* (1990) would later riff brilliantly on the same horrible idea.

Like Ruth, *Repulsion*'s Carol appears completely at odds with the rest of the world, the traumatic events of her earlier life leading to a detachment from normality. The fact that her sister, arguably the closest person to her, cannot see that her faculties are crumbling, and that she is dangerously close to a significant mental collapse, only adds to our frustration. This breakdown in communication is also present in *Prevenge*, Ruth's distancing from reality highlighted not necessarily by the way she dispatches her unfortunate victims but by the way she often struggles to function on a human level in 'everyday' surroundings. This is illustrated during the midwife meetings, when the busy professional is unable to offer true understanding or empathy, instead relying on textbook quotes and verbatim responses.

Ruth's reaction to the world in general is distrust, yet it is never made entirely clear where she and her trauma begin and end. We are never presented with a 'before' version of Ruth in flashback or otherwise, so we are never sure whether her trauma has 'made her' or merely enhanced her misanthropic viewpoint. The fact that she uses the loss of her partner as motivation for her murder spree may just be subterfuge on her part, the strength of their relationship (again something we are never party to) being brought into question during an exchange she has with her final victim: 'I know he was thinking of leaving you.'

This trick of using a female character's fractured viewpoint as filter for our audience perception, to either build empathy or throw us completely off-guard, is one that has been used effectively in numerous 'psychotic women' sub-genre productions. From Hitchcock's *Vertigo* (1958), *Whatever Happened to Baby Jane?* (1962), *Fatal Attraction* (1987), or even underground exploitation films like *The Baby*, it's a trope which occurs repeatedly in modern cinema. Even films like *Psycho* (1960) and *Santa Sangra* (1989) 'borrow' the persona of 'mentally deranged female' and apply it to weaker or 'invisible' male protagonists. Only by 'becoming' his mother, or at least the twisted version of her, does Norman Bates carry out his murders.

Lowe in some respects continues this tradition and yet the bravery and originality of *Prevenge* is in its refusal to pin the protagonist's true motivations down to trite exposition. Ruth's supposed connection with the past in the form of her unborn child, who seemingly guides her into a life of crime, is destroyed in the final moments of the film when she admits that the baby is only a baby, her destructive nature is hers and hers alone.

Andrzej Zulawski's *Possession*, another influence on *Prevenge*, also presents an ambiguous narrative, choosing to frame the ins and outs of a messy relationship break-up with outrageous Lovecraftian imagery, disjointed storytelling and heightened dramatic dialogue. It is also a key example, like *Prevenge*, of a text which dismisses stereotypical representations of motherhood. Isabelle Adjani's Anna appears to show scant regard for her young son, abandoning him when she embarks on a fantastical and disturbing 'relationship' with a slimy tentacled-nightmare which resides in a filthy Berlin apartment. The blue palette, as opposed to the red which permeates *Prevenge* and acts as a signifier of doom in *Don't Look Now*, seems to denote the coldness which invades much of the production. Mark (Sam Neil) and Anna, though in contact with other humans, appear to exist in isolation. The 'world' is something which is beyond their limited focus, blinkered by an all-encompassing separation – a viewpoint many divorcees or children of divorcees will identify with, as David Cronenberg would probably testify.

Anna, like Ruth, also suffers a traumatic loss which comes in the form a protracted 'miscarriage'. One of the most bizarre and uncomfortable scenes committed to camera, it captures an incredible performance by Adjani. Obviously in some pain, Anna, loaded with a shopping bag begins to convulse violently, the laughter which accompanies her agonies only making the sequence more alarming. Soon the small collection of groceries is smashed against the filthy walls of the subway. Milk, like spattering semen, is cast about the dingy confines, the beleaguered character, possessed by some internal force is reduced to Old Testament style throes of madness, bewitched and out of control. Her stockinged feet squirm about in the wet, piss stinking floor, as white fluid and what looks like blood ooze from her mouth and chest. It's stunningly vile and also completely unmissable; at just over three minutes long it feels longer but the fact that we fully engage with our sense of revulsion right to the end is tribute to both Zulawksi and Adjani. Lowe was inspired by the look and feel of *Possession*, and its subway scene is echoed in *Prevenge* – yet where Zulawski shows us an out-of-control character in the relative peace of a deserted tunnel, Lowe gives us Ruth, a calm, collected killer, quietly going about her murderous intent flanked by the growing disturbance of a busy Halloween street scene. Adjani is cast in blue, a cold soul drained of everything, while Lowe, bursting with potential life, becomes a burning red beacon as the night and story grows darker.

Image #6 – Isabella Adjani, Possession *(1981) © Gaumont*

Image #7 – Alice Lowe, Prevenge *(2016) © Western Edge Pictures*

But if *Prevenge*, as with some of the other films mentioned here, successfully plays with our accepted ideas of motherhood, femininity and loss, how might it also subvert the very idea of the traditional horror movie or offshoots like the American slasher?

Chapter 6: Alice Through the Looking Glass

Female homicide has long since been a staple of the horror film. From the very beginnings of cinema, productions sought to depict women as targets of male violence in an endless run of murky *grand guignol* presentations. As early as 1902 we had the French crime thriller *Bluebeard* (1902) – in it, director and ex-magician George Méliès unravels a grim tale of torture and serial killing, replete with a room strewn with the body parts of female victims hanging from meat hooks. This simple but grisly image was repeated over seventy years later in the seminal slasher *The Texas Chain Saw Massacre*. It's perhaps no surprise that these kinds of films were prevalent from such an early time, given that the dawn of the moving image coincided more or less with the recent memories of the 1888 Whitechapel murders in London. Jack the Ripper, a still unknown assailant, who took to the East End streets of London to brutally dispatch five women, has since turned into a cottage industry of walking tours, endless books, TV shows and of course films. Hitchcock's early silent production *The Lodger* (1927) was perhaps the first cinematic cash-in on this horrible series of events. The public obsession with that case, in particular the way in which the focus was primarily on the perpetrator and not Mary Ann Nichols, Annie Chapman, Elizabeth Stride, Catherine Eddowes or Mary Kelly, perhaps tells us something about a kind of ghoulish mindset which was developing and would go on to dominate the burgeoning new cinematic art form.

Thirty-three years after *The Lodger*, the same, much-celebrated director brought us another dark tale of serial murder, one which would change the modern horror film forever. Hitchcock's *Psycho*, undoubtedly heavily influenced by Henri-Georges Clouzot's earlier production, *Les Diaboliques* (1955), was a *tour de force* of beautiful cinematography, brilliant editing and masterful storytelling. Initially focused on female fugitive Marion Crane (Janet Leigh), who has absconded her home town with the boss's money, it's a superbly tense thriller, which becomes more so when the unfortunate Miss Crane pulls up at the Bates Motel. Its tone and presentation would provide the yardstick for future crime features and its brutal delivery meant that many existing horror films began to look a little out of date. The stark black and white, independent feel of the piece stood in stark contrast to the director's other more recent colourful offerings.

The grubby 'reality' which bleeds out of the screen, never more so than in its infamous shower scene, made for a jarring experience for first-time viewers. But had the film been merely about shock value then it's doubtful that scholars would still be talking about it today. What made it stand out was the way in which Hitchcock focuses in on the troubled Norman Bates; despite being party to his terrible crimes by the end of the picture, audiences have learned to know Bates in a way that other movies had never asked them to know a murderer before. Perhaps not since Fritz Lang's *M* (1931) had they been called on to crawl inside a serial killer's head. Not only that, Hitchcock forces cinemagoers to experience Norman (and Marion's) sickening decline in a disturbingly voyeuristic manner. Within the space of its less-than-two-hour run time they have travelled from the bright skies of Phoenix to the depths of a bubbling backwater swamp in the closing seconds of the production. Undoubtedly a classic, *Psycho* remains an important milestone in terms of what audiences would begin to accept and later come to expect in a thriller or horror genre piece. The swish of a velvet cloak or the flap of a rubber bat wing would never have quite the same effect again on audiences who had experienced Norman's hospitality.

By the end of the 1960s, young Americans, whose senses had been dulled by the endless barrage of actual death and destruction brought to them via the daily Vietnam War television updates, had grown weary of the older forms of celluloid scares and were craving something new. That 'new' wave of horror came at them through vehicles like Polanski's *Rosemary's Baby* but more importantly through low-budget blood and gut fest *Night of the Living Dead* (1968). George A. Romero's zombie film, a bleak monochrome siege story that played out in a semi-documentary style, not only challenged viewers in terms of its graphic imagery it also challenged much of the country's less-than-liberal ideas about race and integration. Made in the same year that many cities were experiencing protests or full-on race riots, the casting of a black man as lead may not have been deliberately political but it could certainly be read that way. It opened the doors for other directors too, not only did it reinvent the old voodoo-style, slightly racist zombie movies of the thirties, it also proved that exploitation and more serious social commentary need not necessarily be mutually exclusive. What's more, in some respects it paved the way for a slew of extreme 'maniac killer' films which would become the norm by the early '80s and the dawn of the video nasty. Wes

Craven's *The Last House on the Left* (1972) was a bleak and bizarre murder tale, which according to Zinoman 'shifted the horror movie away from children's entertainment and toward extreme adult scares' (Zinoman, 2012). Though much of that film now appears dated, amateurish and cheap, it is still an uneasy watch – what made it so brutally important and unforgettable at the time was its sickening sense of nihilism. Here were killers whose actions carried no meaning, they simply did what they did because they could. It was a sobering, horrible reflection of an increasingly violent, hopeless society, and through it we can trace the rise of the slasher movie. John Carpenter's *Halloween* (1978), featuring faceless assailant Michael Myers would kick-start a generation of murderous phantoms known only by their mask or shape. Whether it was Jason from *Friday the 13th* (1980), or Leatherface, Cropsie or a host of other copy-cat creations, the bogey-men (and they *are* men) of these movies hacked, slashed and tortured their way through an army of mainly female victims. Though this particular horror sub-genre was undoubtedly an American one, it also owed much the Italian *giallo* movies of the 1960s and '70s.

Giallo movies, so called because they were initially based on the pulpy yellow (*giallo*) covered salacious crime thrillers sold on Italian news stands, became the playgrounds of new and established directors like Mario Bava or Dario Argento. Bava's *The Girl Who Knew Too Much* (1963) arguably became the first solid example of the form; it's intricate storytelling and dreamlike feel owed much to Hitchcock, yet there was something so exactingly European about the style, that it was difficult not to credit it as a uniquely Italian invention. Argento, who had begun as a screenwriter, even providing the script for Leone's *Once Upon a Time in The West* (1968), went on the surpass even Bava with his take on the *giallo* sub-genre. His *The Bird with the Crystal Plumage* (1970) became for many the defining example of that particular kind of movie. The black-gloved killer at the centre of a delicately assembled mystery is an essential element in the *giallo* thriller, yet Argento took this concept and expanded upon it, creating a narrative puzzle which is smashed into pieces and presented to us in a series of seeming non-sequiturs, only to be placed together again in the final moments of the film. The director would, at least for a time, move away from the form, trying his hand at a string of beautifully crafted supernatural horrors such as Deep Red and the unsurpassed *Suspiria* (1977). The *giallo* film could, though, in the hands of less creative filmmakers, descend into more questionable territory; films like Sergio Martino's *Torso* (1973), for instance, became a fairly on-the-nose exemplification of Laura Mulvey's theories (1975) about the 'male gaze', with its scenes of female nudity and sexual titillation laid out against the background of extreme violence.

With the arrival of the American slasher came the now well-established trope of the Final Girl, defined here by Carol J. Clover in *Men, Women and Chain Saws: Gender in the Modern Horror Film*:

> She is intelligent, watchful, and level-headed; the first character to sense something amiss and the only one to deduce from the accumulating evidence the pattern and extent of the threat; the only one, in other words, whose perspective approaches our own privileged understanding of the situation. We register her horror as she stumbles on the corpses of her friends. Her momentary paralysis in the face of death duplicates those moments of the universal nightmare experience – in which she is the undisputed 'I' – on which horror frankly trades. (Clover, 1993)

The character of Laurie (Jamie Lee Curtis) in *Halloween* would perhaps be the archetypal manifestation of this trope; however, she would be unusual in many respects as she was a character that was able to effectively transition from original film to other sequels (though not all). This is not typically the case, as Walter Rankin points out in *Grimm Pictures*:

> … the audience roots for the Final Girl as she stabs, shoots burns, and even beheads the killer. It is important to keep in mind that, while the Final Girl may well survive the final reel, sequels to these films tend to emphasize a disturbing end for her. As the series continues, the killer emerges yet again dispensing with her in the opening scene to make room for the next girl in the cycle. (Rankin, 2007)

Yet, as clearly defined as the trope is, this is not to say that there have not been examples where the concept is subverted or at least presented from a less obvious angle. When Brian De Palma, who had been influenced by both the *giallo* film and Hitchcock, took on the Stephen King adaptation *Carrie* (1976), a pre-*Halloween* supernatural thriller about a troubled teen who is blessed/cursed with telekinetic powers, the anti-hero protagonist is shown as a changeable force, exhibiting altering states of being. Carrie White (Sissy Spacek) presents as more than one character archetype, shifting from being Cinderella-style victim in the first act, to burgeoning Princess in the second, to the monsterous villain in the final scenes. The Final Girl character in *Carrie* could be attributed to Sue Snell (Amy Irving), who exhibits many of the traits defined by Clover; for instance, she certainly is 'the only one to deduce from the accumulating evidence the pattern and extent of the threat', and she is also seen stumbling 'on the corpses of her friends' only to survive the ordeal. However, Carrie also survives beyond the final reel, not physically but in the head of Sue. Her presence in the latter girl's vivid dreams is again a nod to Clover's Final Girl concept: 'Her momentary paralysis in the face of death duplicates those moments of the universal nightmare experience' (Clover, 1993).

Lowe's film is also a subversion on many levels of the more traditional horror film. Ruth, as already discussed, is the antithesis of the Hollywood monster/ slasher trope. Not only does she present us with an unsettling juxtaposed image of a heavily pregnant mother versus psycho killer, she also upends much of what has previously been established by many of the movies mentioned beforehand. *Prevenge*, whether deliberately or not, seems to present us with a twisted reflection of the Norman Bates figure. Just as Hitchcock's killer sought to dress in the garb of a traditional female character – the mother – Ruth's alter-egos seem to move away from the clichéd parent image to the party girl, the Halloween costume, the business-minded professional, all serving to detract from her maternal qualities, not emphasise them in the way that Norman Bates does. She also seeks out her prey in largely public places, her pregnancy allowing her a certain freedom of movement within a society which is unable to recognise her potential threat, whereas Bates is forced to wait spider like in the web of the hotel to carry out his mother's awful bidding. There is also an inversion when it comes to the nature of each character and their supposed forms of possession: Bates chooses to believe his elderly mother is forcing him to commit his crimes, while Ruth is controlled by her unborn daughter. The climax of *Psycho* also becomes a mirror image of *Prevenge*, Ruth is left standing on the top of a cliff – the highest vantage point, while Hitchcock's film ends at the swamp – a symbolic low.

Ruth also refracts the image of *Halloween*'s Michael Myers. Just as Carpenter's supernatural monster becomes a silent killer, on the periphery of our vison, a phantom on the edges of our understanding, who evolves into an inescapable nightmare, Ruth is only too happy to be the centre of attention, employing her chameleon-like quality and communication skills to weave her evil ways. Her 'invisibility' or at least the way in which her dangers remain 'unseen' lay in her pregnant visibility. In one moment, in the seconds after killing one victim, Ruth takes to the streets triumphant, she raises her arms in the air, all powerful. But when she is admonished by her unborn daughter, she shrinks back into an ignored expectant mother. Her face, too, becomes a weapon, while Michael Myer's 'real' face is his only weakness. In another distortion of this figure, Ruth continues to change throughout the narrative, unlike Carpenter's creation which remains an unchangeable shape. Ruth battles with many aspects of her personality and situation. Her first two kills are slightly clumsy, and it is clear that there is an element of doubt or nervousness creeping in. However, by her third murder it is apparent that she has become much more efficient. Ruth never hesitates, she confidently kisses her victim full on the lips before taking a blade to her neck. Her self-assurance has grown so much that she even throws in deeply ironic 'cut-throat business' one liners, both foreshadowing Ella's demise and mocking her earlier boardroom jargon ('I've had to make cuts already – it's been awful'). Lowe inverts another aspect of Carpenter's film – not only is Ruth the 'monster' of the piece, she is also in essence an inverted version of The Final Girl trope. Despite her crimes, she becomes a tragic figure for our sympathy, lives beyond the closing reel, and having recently given birth, she challenges the idea of the surviving female as 'untouched' or 'virginal'.

Like *Prevenge*, William Lustig's low-budget serial killer flick *Maniac* (1980) placed a seemingly unremarkable character at the heart of the madness. Frank Zito, an average blue collar Joe, is able to carry out and get away with his brutal attacks simply because he is someone we walk past on the street without noticing. But when Lustig allows us, or should that be drags us, into his disturbing underworld of murder and psychosis, we become party to Frank's unhinged viewpoints because of the voyeuristic nature of the piece. Like many male serial murderers, Frank collects trophies, his being in the form of female scalps, which he violently nails to the heads of mannequins dressed in the outfits of his victims. Freud's studies on fetishism alert us to the male fear of emasculation, so that we might view Frank's removal of hair/scalps and interpret it as a way of him carrying out the kind of castration he is secretly trying to avoid. Interestingly, Zito, who, like Bates, has serious maternal issues, appears to select his 'trophies', at least partly, based on their aesthetic representation of stereotypical 'feminine' forms. His victims include a nurse, a sex worker and a glamour model. He keeps his mannequins in a tiny dark room, full of mementoes in a hellish candle-lit shrine to his dead mother. By contrast, Ruth keeps no trophies, and in a reversal of Lustig's narrative she becomes a living 'mannequin' figure, presenting herself to different targets as people or 'things' they might understand – the do-gooding charity collector, the after-hours singleton in need of sex, or the heavily made-up ghoul. By doing this she can gain entry to people's homes, parties or workspaces unheeded. Her inner sanctum becomes not a shadowy Bat Cave such as Frank's but the stark interchangeable hotel rooms she returns to after the murders have been committed. While Frank's evil/madness is represented by the physical objects he surrounds himself with, the only visual manifestations of Ruth's insanity (other than her acts) are the glimpses of late-night movie *Crime Without Passion* (1934), which creepily works its way into her consciousness as she lies awake in bed, eating crisps, stating 'I've had mascara days like that'.

Twenty years before *Maniac*, Michael Powell's *Peeping Tom* (1960) followed troubled protagonist Mark as he travelled down his murderous path. What made the production so unnerving at the time, was the way in which Powell forced us to be placed vicariously in the position of Michael. We observe the most violent aspects of his personality, via his viewpoint, thanks to the film's employment of voyeuristic camera work. *Psycho*, released the same year, also employed an uneasy form of voyeurism, yet the nature of the cinematography on *Peeping Tom* does not allow us the same distancing that Hitchcock utilises. Though we may witness some of Bates's crimes 'through his eyes', particularly when he spies on Marion Crane as she strips for her shower, the director also permits us to enjoy the story via the viewpoints of other characters: it is clear that we are not and never can be the film's twisted killer. In the end, he is another cinematic phantom. Powell's film, though, seems to chastise us for our acceptance of this needless violence as entertainment. The lines that are drawn between us and Mark Lewis (Carl Boehm) are far more blurred than they had been in other films. The question of perhaps just how close we are to becoming Mark is uncomfortably explored. Though recognised as a screen classic now, *Peeping Tom* at the time, unlike *Psycho*, was brutally savaged by the critics and the film all but ended Powell's career. Arguably, audiences were not quite ready for the film's honesty about the unexplored nature of our dark humanity.

In some respects, Ruth shares much of her DNA with a character like Mark. She is a lone assailant, she is completely at odds with normal society and she is struggling to get over a past trauma. However, where we are made to check our own possible similarities to Mark in Powell's film, without necessarily feeling any compassion for him, in some sense the opposite is true of Ruth. Lowe deliberately creates a barrier between us and her protagonist, we are never expected to feel or 'see' things from her point of view. And while we might sensibly conclude that this should make the character less sympathetic, in fact it is her complete isolation that draws us closer, so lost is she in her world of pain, that we cannot help but feel some level of empathy, despite her heinous acts or the defence shields she erects. Not only this, it is hinted of in Powell's film that his protagonist's crimes are in part the result of the cruel behaviour inflicted on him by an abusive father. *Prevenge* can be seen again as an inversion of this concept. Ruth is arguably the result of a domineering child, in essence becoming an abusive parent as a result.

As well subverting many aspects of the slasher, *Prevenge* also shares a kinship with a host of other productions, which place the female as lead killer. The likes of *Play Misty for Me* (1971), *Sisters* (1973) and *Friday the 13th* (1980) all adhere to and subvert the sub-genre in some form or other. Though the series would later come to focus on hockey mask-wearing Jason, *Friday the 13th* in its original incarnation placed his grieving mother at the centre of the action. Yet, despite this slight similarity, which presented the aggrieved parent as serial monster, not revealed until the last act, the film bears little in common with *Prevenge*, at least on any thematic or artistic level. Though entertaining, Sean S. Cunningham's movie began life as an unashamed cash-in of Carpenter's *Halloween* and, unlike that film, really offered nothing that would shift the paradigm within the wider horror world. If anything it helped to strengthen certain tropes that were already looking a little tired even at that point. Cunningham, who had earlier produced pornographic films and the highly controversial *The Last House on the Left*, spends much of his film hacking his way through a gang of horny teenagers, who are so throwaway that once they are done away with we quickly forget they were ever there. Of course, the more promiscuous characters are dealt with first and the whole thing rolls out like a slasher film tick box. Yet it would prove to be a tick box which dozens of directors throughout the 1980s and beyond would stick rigidly to, leading to a run of ever-changeable hack-and-slash bogey men vehicles such as *Sleepaway Camp* (1983), *The Burning* (1981) and *Happy Birthday to Me* (1981). Interestingly it would be this kind of work that Cunningham's one-time collaborator Craven would come to rip apart in his '90s scary movie satire *Scream* (1996). Craven had, in fact, already successfully subverted the form on at least two other occasions. *Last House on the Left*, with its deeply unsettling nihilist approach revitalised the modern horror film, while his later *A Nightmare on Elm Street* (1984), though incorporating many of the established tropes, also presented the discerning viewer with a more cerebral, slightly Freudian piece, which tapped into our dreams and sub-conscious fears. Similar to *Prevenge*, Craven places not one mother but a group of them at the heart of his story. We learn that in the past they have taken the law into their own hands and executed local child killer and paedophile Freddy Kruger. Of course, Kruger returns as an unstoppable phantom who lurks in the waking nightmares of his killers' daughters' heads. *Prevenge* can be seen as a strange mash-up of these ideas. While Craven presents the 'mother' as ultimate protector and the 'daughter' as victim, with the 'supernatural force' committing his acts as a means of revenge, Lowe presents the 'mother' not as protector, but as a force of vengeance. The daughter too, at least in Ruth's head, is transposed from innocent victim to Kruger-like supernatural force.

When writing *Prevenge*, Lowe was keen to try and head off any clichéd ideas, addressing the material with an intelligent eye, which was both acutely aware of and wary of the past, in terms of cinema and classic literature and mythology, as she states:

> I'm a big fan of *Fatal Attraction* and have my own feminist reading of it, which has almost nothing to do with the original intent of the filmmakers… In some ways *Prevenge* is what Alex could have become if she hadn't been killed. But from her viewpoint, instead of Michael Douglas'. That film is very symptomatic of 'woman as symbol'. Either the Madonna-esque martyr wife who has little to no personality. Or the witch-like adulteress banshee, who is inevitably much more interesting. It's no coincidence that they use Madame Butterfly in *Fatal Attraction*. You can trace these wronged women back in time to Virgil's Dido, Homer's Circe. And in revenge movies, you have to have the incident which morally validates the horrific violence about to be perpetrated by the hero, who is usually male, and many times has lost his wife and

sometimes kids. *John Wick, Mad Max, Gladiator, Taken, Taken 2* [*laughs*]. These heroes are 'allowed' to do whatever they like because they are 'morally righteous' – again, goes right back to Orestes in lassical mythology. I wanted to turn that on its head. I didn't really want to let the audience off the hook by just going, 'Aw, poor thing, she can't help it. She's lost her boyfriend.' I deliberately delayed the knowledge of why Ruth's doing what she's doing because I didn't want to morally mitigate her actions like all those Hollywood blockbusters (Lowe, 2019)

Though *Prevenge* upends the ideas of many horror films of the past, supplanting the dominant male-led narrative with a more feminist counter narrative, how does it compare or sit alongside more recent genre pieces of the twenty-first century?

Chapter 7: Bleeding the Way

> My passions were all gathered together like fingers that made a fist. Drive is considered aggression today. I knew it as purpose.
> *The Lonely Life: An Autobiography*, Bette Davis (1962)

In *The Monstrous Feminine*, Barbara Creed asserts that the witch is defined as

> …an abject figure in that she is represented within patriarchal discourses as an implacable enemy of the symbolic order. She is thought to be dangerous and wily, capable of drawing on her evil powers to wreak destruction on the community. The witch sets out to unsettle boundaries between the rational and irrational, symbolic and imaginary…(Creed, 1993)

It would be an overreach to describe Ruth from *Prevenge* as a witch, however, she certainly is, in some respects, an 'abject figure', and she can also be viewed as an 'implacable enemy of the symbolic order'. Her changeable attitude to her murderous ways, coupled with the 'bewitching' nature of her many disguises, and the exploitation of her pregnant state in order to 'place a spell' on her intended victims, lands her well within the arena of Creed's definition. In over a century of filmmaking the witch has played an important role in a host of horror- and/or fantasy-style productions. From Disney animated features like *Snow White and the Seven Dwarves* (1937) to Nicolas Roeg's *The Witches* (1990), Mario Bava's pre-*giallo* effort *Black Sunday* (1960), or Dario Argento's *Suspiria*, the witch has been variously presented as harbinger of evil, all conquering power and occasionally misunderstood victim. Yet the 'othering' of that kind of figure with its heavily implied 'othering' of gender and feminist thinking, is often all too apparent when studying this 'archetype' and subsequent representations on the silver screen and beyond.

However, certain cinematic outings have presented us with more interesting perspectives, or have at least sought to challenge or engage in a less formulaic manner. In the early part of the last century, Benjamin Christensen's Swedish-Danish production *Häxan* (1922) attempted to examine the witch as a historical figure, his documentary-style feature detailing how women have been tortured and imprisoned or worse in the name of witchcraft. At the time, it was the most expensive Scandinavian production of its kind, and watching *Häxan* today is still an extraordinarily odd experience. Its debauched scenes of Satanic worship and midnight rituals are still genuinely unsettling, their lurid imagery juxtaposing nervously with its silent movie presentation. Yet as entertainingly bizarre as it is, particularly when viewed with the William S. Burroughs voice-over on the American cut of the film, it feels, even now, like an exploitation piece, because it clearly is. Though Christensen's intentions arguably come from a good place, the end result presents us with a narrative which appears to shift the focus from the undoubted cruelty of a power mad patriarchy back onto the shoulders of the 'hysterical' woman. Unlike *Häxan*, however, Michael Reeves's *Witchfinder General*, another exploitation piece fairly relentless in its depiction of violence inflicted on female characters, makes no bones about presenting us with a brutal critique of ruthless patriarchal control. No hint of actual witchcraft is ever proffered, its 'witches' instead incidental victims demonised at the behest of opportunist con-man Matthew Hopkins. Vincent Price is menacingly effective in the lead, and the overall production is both graphically callous and also heartfelt in its intention.

George A. Romero, still fresh from his *Night of the Living Dead* zombie hit, returned with the more sedate *Season of the Witch* (1973). In it, middle-aged housewife Joan Mitchell (Jan White), attempts to escape the confines of early '70s domestic trappings, and her violent domineering husband, by turning to witchcraft. Though not as sensational as Romero's other horror outings, it is remarkably frank and intelligent in its separation from the more normal (for the time) representations of female characters. Though described by the director as a 'feminist' film, the nature of the societal problems highlighted were brought ironically to the fore when (out of the control of Romero), early cuts of the film were re-edited and sold as soft pornographic feature, *Hungry Wives*. More recently, the archetype has been given a more ambiguous representation in the Robert Eggers production *The Witch* (2015). Set in the seventeenth century it focusses on a puritan family of English settlers who have been abandoned by their original colony. It deals with the hardships and dangers of trying to survive in the harsh environment of an 'uncivilised' America, in an odd reflection of modernity, given the US's recent explosions of race hatred, civil disobedience and Trumpism, but more importantly it centres on the idea of witchcraft as either being real or imagined. Though Eggers never makes it clear whether the 'magic' on screen is actual (i.e. within the reality of the narrative) or hallucinatory, the mixing together of gritty realism with flights of fancy, provides us with an unsettling sense of unease as we shift between judgements which veer between the rational and the nightmarish. Its Salem-inspired story, replete with infant mortality, rotting crops and isolation, manages to make us feel claustrophobic one minute, in the family's darkly repressive living quarters and then completely lost in the vastness of the foreign wilderness in the next.

Perhaps the most visually stylistic recent take on the witch was Anna Biller's *The Love Witch*. Released the same year as *Prevenge*, Biller, like Lowe, presents us with something familiar, a classic timeless piece that is shown to us via the filter of today. As she stated when interviewed by *Diabolique Magazine*:

> This film really comes from my interest in creating a cinema for women, but to also make films that are noteworthy additions to the horror genre. I want to have female protagonists, feminine consciousness and a female point of view. I also wanted to create a femme fatale character who embodies the stereotypes, contradictions, and problems of female consciousness and male projection. The witch is a really interesting figure for me. She embodies a real woman's power and dignity, but also represents all these crazy male projections throughout history: she's evil, her sexuality is evil, she's just a male fantasy of what is evil in women. She has become a scapegoat and a poison container of what men want to disavow, their own feelings of fear, fear of female power and goddess power. (Biller, 2016)

Like Ruth, female protagonist Elaine (Samantha Robinson) is a vengeful killer. But whereas Ruth in part uses preconceived ideas of pregnancy and vulnerability to lure her victims, Elaine, who targets only men, uses patriarchal stereotypes of womanhood as weapons. Flaunting her obvious beauty and combining it with superlative housekeeping skills, perfect clothes and unhampered sexuality, she is able to break her 'conquests' easily with potions and various other forms of control. Also like Lowe, Biller gives us constant reminders of the female body's link to nature in all its bloody reality. But where Ruth in *Prevenge* seems somewhat reluctant to admit to being part of the 'natural way of things', jokingly admonishing nature as 'a bit of a cunt', Elaine seems to embrace it. In one scene, she casually buries her latest victim with a small jar containing, some herbs, her urine and a used sanitary product, noting that

Tampons aren't gross. Women bleed and that's a beautiful thing. Do you know that most men have never even seen a used Tampon?

Image #8 Samantha Robinson, The Love Witch (2016) © Anna Biller Productions

In fact, as A.O. Scott noted in his *New York Times* review, as in *Prevenge*, blood or at least symbolic representations of such, supplies an important colourful flourish:

> *The Love Witch* is, among other things, a study in the color red. Elaine, whose vocation is succinctly captured in the title of Anna Biller's new film, is first seen driving north from San Francisco in a bright red convertible with a matching set of luggage in the back seat and a slightly contrasting shade of lipstick on her mouth and on the stubbed-out cigarettes in the car's ashtray. Later on, red wine will be spilled, and there will be blood from various sources. (Scott, 2016)

And it is scenes like the tampon moment which separate the film from merely being a pitch-perfect visual tribute to 1960s and early '70s features like *The Mephisto Waltz* (1971), *Season of the Witch* or indeed a host of Italian *giallo* movies. Which is not to say that Biller doesn't do a phenomenal job with the detailed styling of the piece. Every aspect of it from its vintage colouring, make-up, costume, set design and choice of locations has been utilised in an unerringly fastidious fashion. Yet, like *Prevenge* it is a distinctly modern film, which seems to reject lazier representations of adult female characters, and also doesn't seem to want to us to make a moral judgement about a clearly unhinged murderer.

However, Elaine and Ruth in some respects belong to different universes. Lowe's naturalistic staging coupled with the more kitchen sink aspects and the smaller-than-life nature of the protagonist, jars when placed against Biller's much more flamboyant pastiche. It might be easy to mistake both texts as singing different songs. Lowe's work feels like an early hit by The Smiths, and Biller's *The Love Witch* provides us with a Phil Spector-like 'Wall of Sound'. But both productions give us carefully observed twenty-first-century viewpoints. Despite the subtler influences which are present in Lowe's film and the more obvious stylisation of Biller's piece, each production rejects the kind of romanticised or demonised form of feminism, and their individual social vistas are projected with minimal interference from skewed male or hegemonic framing.

Though both films lean toward more feminist narratives, neither effort, at least within the proximities of their immediate stories, offer us any form of unquestioned sisterhood. The 'power' of each personality, comes not through an enforced sense of politically correct togetherness, but in fact is drawn from each character's respective ability to stand utterly alone. Neither Ruth in the hands of Lowe, or Elaine in the hands of Biller is expected to 'do the right thing' simply because they are female. Elaine not only sleeps with her neighbour Trish's husband, she also taunts her by pretending to be her friend. Ruth, too, avoids this clichéd response, being just as keen to obliterate female as well as male victims. She initially holds no truck with her 'supportive' midwife, and wanders like a ghost through accepted forms of 'normal' communicative states.

Each film also exists within its own otherworldliness – over and above the accepted closed romantic realism of most cinematic presentations. Though this slightly removed dreamscape is all the more noticeable in Biller's film with its rich palette and detailed period stylings, it is also present in *Prevenge*. Ruth arguably exists in a foggy fantasy of her own creation; like Elaine in the final bloody moments of *The Love Witch*, or even Travis Bickle in *Taxi Driver*, she remains wilfully lost and unapologetically deluded.

The witch or archetypal mother were not the only familiar tropes to be given a twenty-first-century make-over from a distinctly female point of view. Two years before the release of either *The Love Witch* or *Prevenge*, Ana Lily Amirpour bought us a stark and beautiful, radically different take on arguably the oldest cinematic horror figure of them all, the vampire.

Taking its visual cues from the likes of F.W. Murnau's *Nosferatu* (1922) and Jim Jarmusch's *Stranger than Paradise* (1984), *A Girl Walks Home Alone at Night* (2014) is a wonderfully strange, visually arresting, modern black and white presentation, incorporating '80s pop references, nods to '50s teen classics like *Rebel Without a Cause* (1955) and Islamic tradition. Of course, there had been earlier depictions of female vampires including *Dracula's Daughter* (1936), a sultry Universal horror dripping with lesbian sub-text, which in turn influenced the later *Daughters of Darkness* (1971), *Countess Dracula* (1971) and, of course, Tony Scott's sublime *The Hunger* (1983). Yet though all these examples, as well as more recent efforts such as *Let the Right One In* (2008), place the woman/female blood sucker at the forefront of the action, they are positioned within the realms of male-dominated productions and narratives. However, Ana Lily Amirpour's film, like the work of Biller or Lowe which would follow, paints a richer, more abstract picture, which although not overtly feminist as commonly understood (in fact, the director refuses to be drawn in to such debates), creates a wholly new version of a tired genre legend, subverting gender and cultural expectations, which in itself becomes vaguely political.

Amirpour, though born in England, moved with her family of Iranian heritage to Miami when she was still young, and this mix of influences, cultures and viewpoints blends together in a marvellously erratic fashion in her debut feature. Describing it as an 'Iranian spaghetti western vampire film' it's a dreamy vision of comic-book-like storytelling winding in elements of expressionism and Lynchian delights. Amirpour's protagonist, known only as 'The Girl' is a skateboard-riding creature of the night decked out in full *hijab* and western-style trainers. Though more enigmatic, like Ruth in *Prevenge* she also becomes a more complex entity, refusing to adhere to our preconceptions. The Girl (Shelia Vand) is as romantic as she is utterly ruthless, between bouts of vampirism she amuses herself in the pop cultural *mise-en-scène* of her tiny garret-like bedroom, carefully applying goth-style make while listening to 1980s new wave tunes. Amirpour's direction, when coupled with Lyle Vincent's stunningly crisp monochrome cinematography, constructs a remarkably addictive filmic spell channelling Nicholas Ray and *Eraserhead*. As in *Prevenge* and *The Love Witch*, *A Girl Walks Home Alone at Night* places the female lead squarely in charge of the proceedings. Male character Arash (Arash Marjandi), very much cast in the shadow of the late James Dean, either becomes The Girl's willing accomplice or love interest, it's never really made clear which. Interestingly Arash's father's addiction to heroin is, within the context of the story, presented as male weakness while The Girl's addiction and requisition of human blood is played out as an exhibition of power. Blood again becomes an important counterpoint, underlining the film's female viewpoint, and while we don't see it used as symbolic colour coding as in *Prevenge* or *The Love Witch*, its presence is never too far removed from our thoughts. Indeed, posters for all three productions feature blood, or at least hints of blood in their respective designs. The image for *Prevenge*, as discussed previously, is dominated by red, while the ad campaign for *A Girl Walks Home Alone at Night* highlights the protagonist's scarlet lips in a simple Saul Bass-style design, and *The Love Witch* poster portrays Elaine resplendent in satin sheets, blood dripping from her beautifully manicured finger nails. And while blood or a symbolic red can be seen merely as a signifier of horror, it's hard not to see it as being deliberately akin to female issues and womanhood, particularly when placed alongside another contemporary non-horror feature, *Funny Cow* which also uses a red palette to relate its angry female protagonist's story arc.

Though each of these films survives on its own merits, it could be suggested that there is a kinship between each protagonist, but especially between Ruth and Elaine. Though Ruth arguably stands more rigidly within the context of the 'normal', at least from a stylistic standpoint, and while she is technically not a witch nor a vampire (though her late-night Halloween trawl through the Cardiff streets, lends her a Nosferatu-like quality), she does exist within the twilight world. Both she and Elaine appear to survive in the gaps which are created between reality and the unreal. We can read *The Love Witch*, for example, and its meticulously crafted design which is both a perfect mimicry and parody of a dated and vaguely sexist 1960s film world, as a fracturing representation of Elaine's collapsing sanity. This strange fantasy which surrounds her is perhaps merely the way in which she processes the world, to justify her actions and this is exposed slightly in the closing seconds of the film when we begin to see cracks in her tragic illusionary status.

In *Prevenge*, Ruth's own brand of rage and nihilism is distilled into the personality of her unborn daughter. This device, of course works well from a horror film point of view – exploiting the well-trodden trope of monstrous child – but it also serves another purpose. As Lowe explains:

There is conflict there, as it goes on, you start to realise that the baby really represents all of that kind of nihilistic expression, you know, and this very hard line, and really Ruth has much more humane instincts which is why she kisses them [the victims] and stuff, and why she has some doubt and nerves. Especially the pet shop owner, who's supposed to be her first kill, so she definitely has a reaction to that of… 'What have I done?', slightly. (Lowe, 2020)

In essence, *Prevenge* might be read as a possession film for most of its running time, allowing Ruth to be seen as part-victim. And yet, when Ruth's delusion is tragically shattered, when her child turns out to be a normal kid, she chooses not sad reflection or guilt but embraces a new form of freedom, redoubling her murderous intentions in a triumphant climax. Ultimately *Prevenge*, is more tragic than it is comic. Though the comedy works incredibly well, in the end patrons are more likely to leave the cinema with sadness above any other emotion. This is, after all, a film about the grieving process, one that also details a single woman's descent into mental health difficulties. Lowe wrote much of the script while going through the 'teary' phase of the first trimester, and the tone of the piece would seem to reflect this. As Lowe goes on to say:

> …Yeah, you don't feel particularly like sunshine and flowers…especially if you've not experienced depression before, I think some women do experience depression for the first time ever when they're pregnant. They feel a sense of doom and like a sense of negativity in that first trimester and that's something that people don't really talk about. They're just a bit, 'Ooh she's crying a bit because she's pregnant', you know? But it can feel a lot more serious than that. When I was, pregnant and didn't know, I thought I had cancer, I was convinced I had cancer…I just though something's wrong here, I don't know what it is but I'm probably dying…(Lowe, 2019)

Yet, whether we see *Prevenge* as a simple comedy horror film – it is after all, laugh-out-loud funny in places – or a parable about the 'loss of self' experienced while pregnant, or even as a bloody slasher vehicle, what can't be overlooked is its intelligence, its urgency and its originality. What *Prevenge* does, in an increasingly rare sense, is shift the paradigm, particularly when it comes to representation of women, motherhood and pregnancy. And while, largely because of its cult status and failure to initially set the box office on fire, it doesn't so much throw open the door as leave a small crack, in this way, it still remains an important piece of work.

Its originality lies not only in the way that Lowe as female director, actor and writer (still sadly a comparative rarity in a male dominated film-industry) controls the project so competently and thoroughly, but also in its subject matter and delivery thereof. As discussed at length beforehand what Lowe does via her story of motherhood and murder is award a form of agency to a pregnant character, a heavily pregnant one at that, almost unheard of in other films. Never does she allow Ruth to descend into the helpless victim or become the kind of killer who is only a thinly veiled automaton as seen in earlier slasher monster/movies. We may not like Ruth but we cannot deny she is there and that we have some idea of who she is. We can hate her, understand her or chastise her but we cannot ignore her.

Though there may be obvious comparisons we can make to other films including the work already examined in this book, *Prevenge* remains a show of its own making. It may dip into the past at times and borrow structures we have seen before, but what Lowe does best is infuse her particular projects, especially *Prevenge*, with a personality that appears to be non-transferable. It is difficult to imagine such a project being given justice by another director. It is not that Lowe sees herself as an auteur, in fact she would undoubtedly baulk at the term, and yet in many respects, to some, she has become that with her debut feature. She is an auteur, not in the clichéd sense, but in her practicality, bloody-mindedness and independence. A film like *Prevenge* unquestionably requires a degree of bravery and a certain amount of stubbornness, in order to fly against the more restrictive outside forces. As Lowe states:

> There's a lot of cold feet, you know? Particularly in British television. Like, people go 'We love your voice, we love your ideas, we love this…' and then when it comes to the crunch they go, 'We're not sure we're scared. It's too weird, it's too dark, it's too this, it's too that.' And it gets watered down and that is how you get a bad show or a bad film. It's when it's like it's neither here nor there. You've compromised, basically… And it's really sad when you see something that was an initially a really good idea, that's turned into this chimera of bad ideas and self-doubt. Being made by committee, basically. You're trying to please everyone, so no one gets pleased. And that's just pointless, isn't it? (Lowe, 2019)

Though a sequel to *Prevenge* was mooted, and a script written, it never came to fruition. Lowe, however, continues to work as actor, writer and director. Her next directorial feature (as of writing) will be *Timestalker*. Also produced by Western Edge Pictures, it promises to be a kind of reincarnation rom-com and a 'thrilling tale of misplaced affection, unrequited lust and revenge'. Though delayed initially due to the birth of Lowe's second child, and then in hiatus due to Covid lockdown restrictions, the film is at the time of writing entering into its pre-production phase.

This book has looked at the creation, production and societal context of a film called *Prevenge*. It has examined, at least in part the world in which it was borne out of and explored the nature of its primary maker's impetus and drive. It has attempted to proffer discussions which link the film to other creative sources and to establish the importance of its existence within a twenty-first-century setting. However, it feels only fitting to leave the last word to Lowe herself:

> It was just liberating to be able to go, I've made all these decisions and they are the right decisions. In the past I think I've made stuff where I was like, yeah, I was never quite happy with that but someone made me doubt myself, so I backtracked and I compromised. I think *Prevenge* was the first time I'd ever gone with my instincts and my instincts were right. And I now try and carry that forward when I'm meeting other people. When I'm pitching stuff, I'm thinking *they don't know, they don't know really know*. (Lowe, 2019)

Sources

Bibliography

Appignanesi, L. (2008) *Mad, Bad and Sad: A History of Women and the Mind Doctors From 1800 to the Present*, Virago Press, London.

Brosnan, J. (1991) *The Primal Screen: A History of Science Fiction Film*, Orbit Books, London and Sydney

Edited by Chibnall, S and Petley, Julian. (2002) *British Horror Cinema*, Routledge, London.

Creed, Barbara. (1993) *The Monstrous Feminine: Film, Feminism, Psychoanalysis*, Routledge, London.

Cronenberg, D. (1992) *Cronenberg on Cronenberg*, Faber and Faber Ltd, London.

Davis, B. (1962) *The Lonely Life: An Autobigraphy*, Hachette Books, New York.

Frank, A.G. (1974) *The Movie Treasury Horror Movies: Tales of Terror in the Cinema*, Octopus Books, London.

Gifford, D. (1973) *A Pictorial History of Horror Movies*, Hamlyn Publishing Group Ltd, Middlesex.

Janiss, L, K. (2012) *House of Psychotic Women*, FAB Press Ltd, Surrey.

King, S. (1981) *Danse Macarbre*, Everest House, New York.

Levin, I. (1967) *Rosemary's Baby*, Corsair, London.

Marriott, J and Newman, K. (2006) *Horror! The Definitive Companion to the Most Terrifying Movies Ever Made*, Carlton Books Ltd, London

McKay, S. (2007) *A Thing of Unspeakable Horror: The History of Hammer Films*, Aurum Press Limited, London.

Mulvey, L. (1975) 'Visual Pleasure and Narrative Cinema', *Screen*, Volume 16, issue 3, pp. 6-18.

Nieland, J. and Niel, J. (2012) *David Lynch*. University of Illinois Press. Urbana, Chicago and Springfield.

Pirie, D. (2008) *A New Heritage of Horror: The English Gothic Cinema*, I.B. Taurus & Co Ltd, London.

Poole, W.S. (2014) *Vampira: Dark Goddess of Horror*, Soft Skull Press, New York.

Rigby, J. (2016) *Euro Gothic: Classics of Continental Horror Cinema*, Signum Books, Cambridge.

Skal, D, J. (1993) *The Monster Show: A Cultural History of Horror*, Plexus Publishing Ltd, London.

Strick, P. (1979) *Science Fiction Movies*, Galley Press, Cathay Books, London.

Wyndham, J. (1957) *The Midwich Cukoos*, Penguin Books, London.

Zinoman, J. (2012) *Shock Value*, Duckworth Overlook, London.

FILMOGRAPHY

10 Rillington Place (1971) [Blu Ray] Directed by Richard Fleischer. UK. Filmways, Genesis Productions

A Girl Walks Home Alone at Night (2014) [Blu Ray] Directed by Ana Lily Amipour. US. Logan Pictures, Spectre Vision.

Alien (1979) [Blu Ray] Directed by Ridley Scott. US. 20th Century Fox

The Babadook (2014) [Blu Ray] Directed by Jennifer Kent. Australia. Screen Australia, Causeway Films

The Baby (1973) [Blu Ray] Directed by Ted Post. US. Quintet productions

Bride of Frankenstein (1935) [Blu Ray] Directed by James Whale. US. Universal Pictures

The Brood (1979) [Blu Ray] Directed by David Cronenberg. Canada. Canadian Film Development Corporation

Don't Look Now (1973) [Blu Ray] Directed by Nicolas Roeg. UK. Casey Productions, Eldorado Films

The Elephant Man (1980) [DVD] Directed by David Lynch. US/UK. Brooks Films, Universal Pictures

Eraserhead (1977) [Blu Ray] Directed by David Lynch. US. American Film Institute

The Exorcist (1973) [Blu Ray] Directed by William Friedkin. US. Warner Bros Pictures

Frankenstein (1931) [Blu Ray] Directed by James Whale. US. Universal Pictures

From Beyond the Grave (1974) [DVD] Directed by Kevin Connor. UK. Amicus Productions, Warner Bros Productions

Funny Cow (2017) [DVD] Directed by Adrian Shergold. UK. Entertainment

Hereditary (2017) [Blu Ray] Directed by Ari Aster. US. A24, PalmStar Media, Finch Entertainment, Windy Hill Pictures

Kill List (2011) [Blu Ray] Directed by Ben Wheatley. UK. Warp X, Rook Films, Film4 Productions, UK Film Council, Screen Yorkshire

The Lodger (1927) [Blu Ray] Directed by Alfred Hitchcock. UK. Gainsborough Pictures

The Love Witch (2016) [Blu Ray] Directed by Anna Biller. US. Anna Biller Productions.

The Man Who Fell to Earth (1976) [DVD] Directed by Nicolas Roeg. UK. British Lion Films

Night of the Living Dead (1968) [Blu Ray] Directed by George Romero. US. Image Ten.

Possession (1981) [Blu Ray] Directed by Andrzej Zulawski. France/West Germany. Gaumont

Prevenge (2016) [Blu Ray] Directed by Alice Lowe. UK. Western Edge Pictures, Gennaker Group, Ffilm Cymru Wale

Psycho (1960) [DVD] Directed by Alfred Hitchcock. US. Shamley Productions

Psychomania (1973) [Blu Ray] Directed by Don Sharp. UK. Benmar Productions

Repulsion (1965) [DVD] Directed by Roman Polanski. UK. Compton Films, Tekli British Productions

Rosemary's Baby (1968) [DVD] Directed by Roman Polanski. US. William Castle Enterprises

Santa Sangre (1989) [DVD] Directed by Alejandro Jodorowksy. Mexico/Italy. Mainland Pictures, Expanded Entertainment

Sightseers (2012) [DVD] Directed by Ben Wheatley. UK: Studio Canal, Big Talk Pictures, Film4 Productions, BFI Film Fund, Rook Films

Tales that Witness Madness (1973) [Blu Ray] Directed by Freddie Francis. UK. World Film Services

The Tenant (1976) [DVD] Directed by Roman Polanski. France. Marianne Productions

The Texas Chainsaw Massacre (1974) [Blu Ray] Directed by Tobe Hooper. US. Vortex

Village of The Damned (1960) [DVD] Directed by Wolf Rila. UK. Metro-Goldwyn-Mayer

Walkabout (1971) [Blu Ray] Directed by Nicolas Roeg. UK/Australia. Max L. Raab-Si Litvinoff Films

Who Can Kill a Child? (1976) [DVD] Directed by Narciso Ibanez Serrador. Spain. American International Pictures

Author Interviews

Lowe, A. (2019, October 25) Skype interview

Lowe, A. (2019, October 8) Email interview

Lowe, A. (2020, February 11) Email interview

Lowe, A. (2020, February 21) Skype interview

Sivell, V. (2019, August 8) Telephone interview

Glover, R. (2020, February 13) Email interview

DVD Interviews

Sightseers (2012) [DVD] Special Feature Interview with Producer Claire Jones, Directed by Ben Wheatley. UK: Studio Canal, Big Talk Pictures, Film4 Productions, BFI Film Fund, Rook Films

Sightseers (2012) [DVD] Special Feature Interview with Alice Lowe, Directed by Ben Wheatley. UK: Studio Canal, Big Talk Pictures, Film4 Productions, BFI Film Fund, Rook Films

Sightseers (2012) [DVD] Special Feature Interview with Ben Wheatley, Directed by Ben Wheatley. UK: Studio Canal, Big Talk Pictures, Film4 Productions, BFI Film Fund, Rook Films

RADIO INTERVIEWS

Houses of Horror, (2015) [Radio Programme] BBC Radio 4: Simon Hollis

PODCASTS

Longworth, K. (2017, March 6) Marilyn Monroe: Dead Blondes Part 6 [Show 98]. *You Must Remember This*. Podcast retrieved from https://www.stitcher.com/podcast/stitcher/you-must-remember-this/e/49356094

ONLINE ARTICLES

Peter Bradshaw, (updated 1 September, 2016), *Prevenge Review: A Mother of a Serial Killer Film*, The Guardian, accessed August 13, 2019 <https://www.theguardian.com/film/2016/sep/01/prevenge-review-alice-lowe-mother-of-a-serial-killer-film>

Jeanette Catsoulis, (updated 22 March, 2017), *Review: 'Prevenge', Orchestrated by a Fiendish Fetus*, The New York Times, accessed August 13, 2019 <https://www.nytimes.com/2017/03/22/movies/prevenge-review.html>

Ryan Lambie, (updated October 10, 2014), *Directing The Babadook*, Den of Geek, accessed March 23, 2020 <https://www.denofgeek.com/movies/jennifer-kent-interview-directing-the-babadook/>

Maitland McDonagh, (updated December, 2013), *Encore: The Baby*, Film Comment, accessed March 23, 2020 <https://www.filmcomment.com/article/encore-the-baby-ted-post/>

Kim Newman, (updated 22 August, 2012), *Sightseers Review*, Empire, accessed December 12, 2019 <https://www.empireonline.com/movies/reviews/sightseers-review/>

Peg Aloi, (updated 27 November 2016), *The Love Witch (2016): An Interview with Writer and Director Anna Biller*, Diabolique Magazine, accessed June 5 2020 <https://

diaboliquemagazine.com/the-love-witch-2016-an-interview-with-writer-and-director-anna-biller/>

Steve Rose, (updated July 12, 2008), *You Don't Know Me*, The Guardian, accessed April 17 2020 <https://www.theguardian.com/culture/2008/jul/12/film.features>

MAGAZINE ARTICLES

Carne, J. (2019) Why Does the Baby Hate Me? Therapy Today Volume 30, Issue 10

Devil's Advocates

"Auteur Publishing's new Devil's Advocates critiques on individual titles offer bracingly fresh perspectives from passionate writers. The series will perfectly complement the BFI archive volumes." Christopher Fowler, Independent on Sunday

THE BLOOD ON SATAN'S CLAW – DAVID EVANS-POWELL

"Evans-Powell has written a powerful and fascinating monograph that is very readable... always relevant and interesting."
Folk Horror Revival

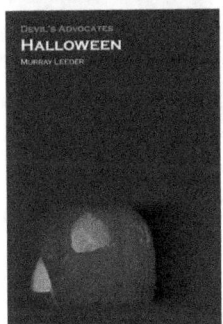

HALLOWEEN – MURRAY LEEDER

"...provides new insights into the social, cultural and cinematic underpinnings, and the stylistic and thematic dimensions, of arguably he most influential scary movie of the last half-century."
Richard Nowell, author of Blood Money (2011)

WITCHFINDER GENERAL – IAN COOPER

"Cooper writes with clarity, wit and confidence, his obvious fondness for the film and for movies in general evident throughout... I read the book in one sitting then returned to it to scour it for any details I might have missed." HorrorTalk

www.ingramcontent.com/pod-product-compliance
Lightning Source LLC
Chambersburg PA
CBHW071414300426
44114CB00016B/2300